SCOTTIS

Editor
DAVID DAICHES

ROBERT FERGUSSON

DAVID DAICHES

SCOTTISH ACADEMIC PRESS

EDINBURGH

Published by
Scottish Academic Press Ltd
33 Montgomery Street, Edinburgh EH7 5JX

821
32,164

First Published 1982
SBN 7073 0305 2

Printed in Great Britain by
Clark Constable Ltd., Edinburgh and London

CONTENTS

ACKNOWLEDGEMENT

The Scottish Academic Press acknowledges the financial assistance of the Scottish Arts Council in the publication of this volume.

CHAPTER I

Walter Ruddiman, nephew of the scholar, printer and librarian Thomas Ruddiman, began to publish *The Weekly Magazine or Edinburgh Amusement* on 7 July 1768: it ran until June 1784. In the issue of 2 January 1772 there appeared in the magazine a poem by Robert Fergusson entitled "The Daft Days". It was unlike anything that had appeared in its pages before. It was a celebratory poem, perpetuating an old Scottish tradition of poems of popular celebration. The Daft Days were the holiday period between Christmas and Handsel Monday (the first Monday of the year), a period which, in spite of Presbyterian frowning on Christmas celebrations as Popish, remained a festive time in Scotland, the emphasis being increasingly put on Hogmanay (the last day of the old year) rather than on Yule (Christmas). Fergusson's poem opens by setting the December scene:

> Now mirk December's dowie face   dark; gloomy
> Glours our the rigs wi' sour grimace,   scowls; ridges
> While, thro' his *minimum* of space,
>   The blear-ey'd sun,
> Wi' blinkin light and stealing pace   flickering
>   His race doth run.

The language is Scots ("mirk", "dowie", "glours", "blinkin") but it is not the patronising or nostalgic rural Scots or the antiquarian Scots of so many writers of Scots verse since the latter part of the seventeenth century. It is an assured, balanced, confident Scots, weighted unostentatiously with a Latin word like *minimum*. It uses an old

stanza form first popularized some hundred and forty
years earlier by Robert Sempill of Beltres in his poem
"Life and Death of the Piper of Kilbarchan", better
known as the "Epitaph of Habbie Simson", a stanza that
Allan Ramsay had accepted earlier as "standard" for a
certain type of Scots poetry. (It had a long history before
Sempill's use of it, and Burns was to develop it from
Ramsay and Fergusson so that today it is often known as
the "Burns stanza".)

Fergusson's poem continues with its winter set-piece:

> From naked groves nae birdie sings,
> To shepherd's pipe nae hillock rings,
> The breeze nae od'rous flavour brings
>   From *Borean* cave,
> And dwyning nature droops her wings,
>   Wi' visage grave.

fading

This is a highly stylised poetry. "Od'rous Flavour" is
not a vernacular expression, neither is the adjective
Borean, while the line

> And dwyning nature droops her wings

has a quiet *gravitas* that shows an assured poet building a
certain formality, a stateliness even, on a foundation of a
direct Scots speech ("nae birdie sings"). The Habbie
Simson stanza, which Sempill of Beltrees used in a self-
consciously rollicking way, and which Ramsay and
Hamilton of Gilbertfield used in a tone of racy vernacular
familiarity in their exchange of verse letters, is here shaped
to strengthen the poet's mood and theme at this point.
The rhymes of "sings", "rings", "brings" and "wings"
help to chime out the sad note of stilled and drooping
nature, while the rhyming short fourth and sixth lines—
standard English except for "wi'" instead of "with"—
anchor the stanza in cold melancholy. This note continues
through the third stanza of the poem, but there is a sudden
shift in the fourth:

> *Auld Reikie*! thou'rt the canty hole,
> A bield for mony caldrife soul,
> Wha snugly at thine ingle loll,
> > Baith warm and couth;
> While round they gar the bicker roll
> > To weet their mouth.

A lively spoken Scots has taken over from the stylised language of the earlier stanzas. "Canty", "bield", "caldrife", "ingle", "couth", "gar the bocker roll" seem to represent a different kind of Scots from "dwyning nature" and a different kind of language altogether from "Borean cave". The transition is in the preceding stanza:

> Mankind but scanty pleasures glean
> Frae snawy hill or barren plain,
> Whan Winter, 'midst his nipping train,
> > Wi' frozen spear,
> Sends drift owr a' his bleak domain,
> > And guides the weir.

The first line of this stanza is in good neo-classic English, the very first word, "mankind", alerting us to a use of generalization one associates with that style. But as the stanza progresses we see an unforced transition to a more direct and vividly mimetic language. Though winter is still personified, with a capital letter and a reference to "*his* nipping train", the adjective "nipping" leaps out of the line with lively force. "Bleak domain" functions equally as neo-classic generalization and specific description of this particular scene, while the Scots "guides the weir" makes the formal picture of Winter with his frozen spear more real and threatening. Then comes the address to Edinburgh ("Auld Reikie"), with the convivial interior contrasting vividly with the frozen scene outside. We have suddenly moved from the winter landscape to the warm fireside where men sit drinking. This contrast between the roughness of the weather outside and the snug interior is

in an old Scottish tradition that goes back at least as far as
the opening of Henryson's *Troilus and Criseyde*.

The poem has now reached its true theme, which is not
the frozen winter landscape but conviviality—brilliantly
localized Edinburgh conviviality. The language is now a
confident and happy Scots:

> When merry *Yule-day* comes, I trow
> You'll scantlins find a hungry mou;
> Sma' are our cares, our stamacks fou
>   O' gusty gear,
> And kickshaws, strangers to our view,
>   Sin Fairn-year.

tasty fare — O' gusty gear

last year — Sin Fairn-year

He can still use the neo-classic personification, but in a
different mood:

> Then, tho' at odds wi' a' the warl',
> Amang oursells we'll never quarrel;
> Tho' Discord gie a canker'd snarl
>   To spoil our glee,
> As lang's there's pith into the barrel
>   We'll drink and 'gree.

Discord is here less a personified abstraction than a real
ill-tempered drunkard giving a "canker'd snarl". And the
line

> As lang's there's pith into the barrel

rings out like a popular proverb.

The patriotic theme emerges naturally from the convivial; when the capital of Scotland celebrates, it must be
in an appropriately Scottish way:

> *Fidlers*, your pins in temper fix,
> And roset weel your fiddle-sticks,
> And banish vile Italian tricks
>   From out your quorum,
> Nor *fortes* wi' *pianos* mix,
>   Gie's *Tulloch Gorum*.

rub with resin — And roset weel your fiddle-sticks

give us — Gie's *Tulloch Gorum*

"Tullochgorum" is the name of a reel tune to which a few years later the Rev. John Skinner of Aberdeen wrote a set of rollicking words, much admired by Burns. Fergusson's touchiness about foreign influences on Scottish music was shown again in his "Elegy, on the Death of Scots Music", which appeared in *The Weekly Magazine* on 5 March 1772. This is a matter to be discussed later: our concern here is with the quality of Fergusson's first published poem in Scots, and its significance as indicating a new development in Scottish poetry.

The concluding stanza of the poem anchors it more solidly than ever in the local Edinburgh scene:

> And thou, great god of *Aqua Vitae*!   whisky
> Wha sways the empire of this city,
> When fou we're sometimes capernoity,   drunk; bad-tempered
>   Be thou prepar'd
> To hedge us frae that black banditti,
>   The City-Guard.

It is a drunken city at this time of the year, and citizens the worse for liquor are liable to have a run-in with the City Guard. The City Guard in eighteenth-century Edinburgh were—as Sir Walter Scott put it in his classic account of them in chapter 3 of *The Heart of Mid-Lothian*— "in general discharged veterans, who had strength enough remaining for this municipal duty, and being, moreover, for the greater part, Highlanders, were neither by birth, education, or former habits, trained to endure with much patience the insults of the rabble, or the provoking petulance of truant schoolboys, and idle debauchees of all descriptions, with whom their occupation brought them into contact." Fergusson seems to have had several encounters with these elderly Highland policemen; at any rate, as Scott says, he "mentions them so often that he may be termed their poet laureate". Their mention here, however, in the very last words of the poem, roots the poem in Edinburgh with absolute specificness.

The first three stanzas show a rural scene, that might be anywhere in Scotland; the fourth introduces Edinburgh as a cosy urban shelter from the wild forces of nature in winter; the penultimate stanza enlarges the sense of celebration to something more general:

> Let mirth abound, let social cheer
> Invest the dawning of the year . . .

in a standard, generalizing, abstract neo-classic English, and then the final stanza localizes the poem again, more firmly than ever, concluding not only with a mention of a specific and well-known Edinburgh phenomenon, the City Guard, but showing by rhyming "Guard" with "prepar'd" that the word is to be pronounced as in Edinburgh Scots.

This, then, is not merely a poem of urban low life such as Allan Ramsay produced in his "Elegy on Lucky Wood" and "Lucky Spence's Last Advice", both written in an aggressive Scots vernacular, a deliberately "vulgar" tongue for a vulgar subject, but a poem that uses the resources of both English and Scots to move with confidence between the general and the particular. It is a poem linked to the old Scottish tradition of poems of revelry and popular celebration though it is not an imitation of any of these and represents an original development. Its author was born in Edinburgh on 5 September 1750 and was thus only twenty-one years old when the poem appeared in *The Weekly Magazine*. How did he come to write poems of this kind and what was the cultural context in which his poetic imagination and his poetic craft worked?

These are not easy questions to answer, for the Scottish poetic tradition underwent some curious and disturbing changes in the two hundred years before Fergusson arrived on the scene. The great age of the Makars, the age of Henryson and Dunbar and Gavin Douglas, when Scots was a rich literary language firmly based on a living speech but absorbing strength and ornamention freely and boldly from English, Latin, French and other European sources, an age when the Scots poet was simultaneously at home in Europe and unselfconsciously aware of his own cultural roots—that age slipped away steadily under the impact of political and religious forces that hastened anglicisation and produced uncertainty about national and cultural identity. The Reformation Parliament of 1560 was a decisive event. Three years after its crucial session the Reformed Church assumed control over printers that had previously been the prerogative of the Crown, so that when George Bannatyne in 1568 compiled his five-volume "Ballat Buik"—"an index of taste and tradition in mid-century Scotland" as Helena Shire has called it[1]—he did not seek publication for it, even though the Reformation had already affected in some degree the way in which the collection was chosen and organized: to quote Mrs. Shire again, the Bannatyne Manuscript "resembles a two-way mirror, reflecting in one direction the courtly making of the past, in another the age of change." It preserves the tradition of courtly love lyric and other varieties of court poetry (closely associated with music) while also including "ballatis detesting of luve and lichery". It does not include devotional poetry, such as hymns to the Virgin, which formed part of the pre-Reformation poetic heritage. It does not, of course, include folk poetry either, although there existed a tradition of popular poetry side by side with the courtly tradition in sixteenth century Scotland, represented not only by poems of popular revelry such as "Peblis to the Play" and "Christis Kirk on the Grene" (both of which have been attributed to James V and suggest therefore a deliberately humorous and even condescending look at folk festivals rather than a spontaneous popular example of such activity) but also by those popular songs which, together with the words of courtly

part-songs, were deliberately parodied into Protestant
religious expression by the brothers Wedderburn of
Dundee probably in the early 1640s in the collection
generally known as the *Gude and Godlie Ballatis*. The
eighteenth-century collector of Scottish songs and
ballads, David Herd, friend of Fergusson and fellow-
member of the Cape Club, printed in the second volume of
his *Ancient and Modern Scottish Songs, Heroic Balads, Etc*.

> John, come kiss me now, now, now,
> O John come kiss me now,
> John come kiss me by and by
>   And make nae mair ado.
>
> Some will court and compliment,
>   And make a great ado,
> Some will make of their goodman,
>   And sae will I of you.
>   John come kiss, &c.

Herd had recovered the original of a popular love song
which the *Gude and Godlie Ballatis* had turned to religious
edification. It appears there in this form:

> Johne, cum kiss me now,
> Johne, cum kis me now;
> Johne, cum kis me by and by
> And mak no moir adow.
>
>   The Lord thy god I am
> That Johne dois the call;
> Johne representit man,
> Be grace celestiall.

It goes on in the vein of the second stanza for another
twenty-four stanzas. Or consider the refrain of a
Protestant anti-papal song in the *Gude and Godly Ballatis*:

> The Paip, that pagane full of pryde,
>   He hes us blindit lang;
> For quhair the blind the blind dois gyde,

Na wonder baith ga wrang;
Like prince and king he led the ring
Of all iniquitie:
Hey trix, tryme go trix,
Under the grene wod-tre.

"Trixie" is the traditional pipe-tune that is mentioned in Sempill's "Epitaph of Habbie Simson" as one of the tunes that will no longer be played now that the piper is dead.

So even at the time when Bannatyne compiled his manuscript there was both a tradition of court poetry (song and music) and of popular poetry (and song) existing side by side. It is thus not true to say that the popular tradition surfaced only after the permanent removal of the Court from Edinburgh when James VI inherited the throne of England to go south to reign as James I of England and govern Scotland, as he boasted, by his pen. It is true that the removal of the Court to England deprived Scotland at a blow of the major if not the only source of patronage of the arts and produced a rapid decline of the sophisticated courtly tradition of poetry and music of which James himself, in poetry at least, had worked hard to encourage a renaissance during his years as King of Scotland only. It is also true that the folk tradition emerged to replace the court tradition when the latter disappeared. But the popular tradition had itself suffered at the hands of the reformers, who had a deep suspicion of popular festivities and of the songs and ballads that accompanied them, associating such things with popery and (accurately enough) even with pre-Christian pagan celebrations. A reading of the minutes of Edinburgh Town Council in the years after 1560 will show this. Thus on 17 November 1587 the Council expelled from the burgh "all menstrallis, pyperis, fidleris, common sangsteris, and specially of baldrie and filthy sangs, and siclyke all vagabonds and maisterless persouns". Popular poetry and music are associated with vice and an avoidance of honest work.

So the folk tradition was under attack in Scotland from the time the reformers became active; some folk literature was driven underground, some was re-baptised, as it were, into the reformed faith as in the *Gude and Godlie Ballatis*; much survived in fragments, choruses, airs (known in England as "Scotch airs" and admired for their popular liveliness) to which both English and Scottish writers wrote new words, and in titles associated with airs which again called forth new words to old titles. It was this fragmented folk tradition that provided an alternative to the court tradition that was lost after 1603. It was to this tradition that many Scots editors and poets and amateurs of literature turned in the early eighteenth century in a self-conscious attempt to promote or at least exhibit a Scots literary tradition that could compensate them for the loss of political identity that resulted from the Union of 1707.

The attempt to rediscover a native literary tradition in a fit of hurt national pride was itself an indication that something had gone wrong with that tradition, for there was a sense of finding and defining something that had been lost. But of course there had been continuity of a kind. The tradition of court poetry and music lingered on in some areas of Scotland, particulary in the north-east, while the "Habbie Simson" tradition mediated in some degree between the old poetry of popular festivities and the new more self-conscious vernacular celebration of such festivities. If the use of Scots was becoming increasingly what could be called "vernacular" (a vernacular being distinguished from a full-blooded literary language by being acknowledged as a local or regional dialect as opposed to the accepted standard language of writing and cultured speech) this was the result of a series of historical events that had begun with the Reformation. The Reformation had separated Scotland from her old ally Catholic France to turn her towards Protestant England; John Knox wrote his *Historie of the Reformatioun* in a deliberately Anglicised Scots because he wanted an English audience; the version of the Bible—first the Geneva Bible then the Authorised Version—in use among Scottish Protestants were English versions, so that standard English (of a rather antiquarian variety) became the language of the pulpit and of deliberately edifying speech. (Burns was well aware of this, as he shows in his "Cotter's Saturday Night" and in the passage in standard English, beginning "But pleasures are like poppies spread", which he interpolates as a mock-moralising outburst in the otherwise racy Scots language of "Tam o' Shanter".) James VI's departure with his Court in 1603, taking his court poets with him, represented another stage in the decline of Scots as a full-blooded literary language. The enormous prestige of Elizabethan and Jacobean English literature was another factor, though this in itself would not have affected literary Scots in that way any more than the prestige of Chaucer turned the Makars away from Scots—it helped to enrich their Scots, not de-nature it. Then the Union of 1707, coming on top of these other developments, speeded further a process well under way. By this time English was firmly established as the language of published prose discourse in Scotland, the language to be learned at school as the accepted educated mode of utterance, and as the language of those poets who sought an English audience, so much larger and richer and more influential than a Scots one.

There was still a Scots poetry, of a kind, being produced, mostly self-consciously rustic, or comically vernacular, or antiquarian. In broadsheets and chap-books some older Scots poetry was still available, generally in debased or fragmented form. And it was to Scots poetry that frustrated Scottish nationalists turned at the time of the Union and after. In 1706, when the passing of the Act of Union already looked inevitable, the deeply patriotic Edinburgh printer James Watson brought out the first of his three volumes entitled *A Choice Collection of Comic and Serious Scots Poems both Ancient and Modern*, with a prefatory note explaining that this first collection of poems "in our native *Scots* dialect" was an attempt to show what Scotland could do in competition with the many English collections of miscellaneous poems. With its mixture of poems of popular revelry, laboured exercises in courtly English, macaronics, mock elegies, serious sixteenth-century Scots poems, trivial epigrams and epitaphs, poems by Drummond of Hawthornden and Montrose, flyting, laments and miscellaneous patriotic pieces, Watson's collection appears at first sight to represent the casual putting together of whatever the editor found to his hand. Yet (except for ballads, which it lacks, and song lyrics, which are few, and the perhaps surprising lack of anything by Sir David Lindsay) the collection represents with a fair degree of accuracy the different kinds of material available for the development or reconstruction of the Scottish poetic tradition in the eighteenth century. The tradition of the Makars as it developed in its last phase was represented by Alexander Montgomerie (?1545–?1610), especially by his remarkable long allegorical poem "The Cherrie and the Slae" with its complex musical stanza which was thus made available to eighteenth-century Scottish poets. (We must wait until Allan Ramsay's *The Ever Green*, 1724, for examples of the earlier Makars.) The courtly tradition in English was represented by William Drummond of Hawthornden (1585–1649), who stayed in Scotland and wrote for the most part in an Elizabethan English idiom, and Sir Robert Aytoun (1569–1638), one of James VI's court poets who followed him to England in 1603 and henceforth wrote in English. The older popular tradition is here, with "Christis Kirk on the Grene", and the new "Habbie Simson" and other pieces. Various kinds of popular and semi-popular Scottish song are represented, some in Scots and some in English. Characteristic forms of

Scottish humour and Scottish violence are represented in various ways (such as "The Flyting between Polwart and Montgomerie"), as is the goliardic tradition as it developed in Scotland and the tradition of macaronic humour (mixed Latin and English) associated with it. Watson printed the best texts he could find, though these were often poor broadsides. Perpetuation in broadsides at least denotes vitality. Throughout the seventeenth century the line between folk song and "art" poem was often obscured in Scotland; poems even by courtly poets found their way to popular singers and printers of broadsides, as well as to private collectors; and changes, corruptions, emendations and additions were the natural result. What Watson printed was far from a representative anthology of great Scottish poetry. But he built some bridges, and made possible a tradition of eighteenth-century Scottish poetry of a kind. The concern with collecting, editing, imitating and annotating Scottish popular poetry, which was to go on right through the eighteenth and early nineteenth centuries, and is manifested by, among others, Allan Ramsay, David Herd and Walter Scott, began as a nostalgic patriotic reaction to the Union. Without that concern neither Fergusson (though he was not at all a folk poet) nor Burns (who was far from being only a folk poet, for all the strength he drew from the folk tradition) would have been possible.

Watson's patriotic anthologising was not the only literary response called forth by the national trauma of the Union. The north-east, especially Aberdeen, preserved a tradition of Humanist (in the Renaissance sense), Jacobite, Episcopalian thought and feeling that was brought to Edinburgh when the Banffshire-born and Aberdeen-educated Thomas Ruddiman (1674–1757) came from Aberdeen to Edinburgh at the turn of the century as a result of his meeting with Dr. Archibald Pitcairne, the Edinburgh physician and poet whose Latin verses represented an attempt to revive the old Scottish

Humanist tradition of which the greatest exponent had
been James VI's tutor George Buchanan. In association
with the Edinburgh scholar-printer Robert Freebairn,
Ruddiman became involved in what has been called
"patriotic editing", of which the most notable examples
were the *Opera Omnia* of Buchanan and Gavin Douglas's
translation of Virgil's *Aeneid*, published by Freebairn with
a glossary of Douglas's Scots by Ruddiman. The
movement led by Ruddiman and Freebairn could be
called vernacular Humanism: its aim was a Scoto-Latin
culture, recognizing older Scots as a great literary
language but looking to a revived Latin as Scotland's
modern literary language before the world. It was thus
quite different from that movement which associated the
use of Scots with ignorance of Latin (as Ramsay and
Burns were to associate it) and saw it as a popular dialect
or vernacular amusement. The movement, which was
strong in Edinburgh in the second, third and fourth
decades of the eighteenth century, was eventually
swamped by the Scottish Enlightenment which sought to
establish Scotland's intellectual precedence by facing
Europe in English dress (as the later eighteenth-century
literati did) although with Scottish intellectual strength.
But although the movement we call vernacular
Humanism did not survive, it left permanent traces.
Fergusson came under its influence, as Burns did not.
Educated at Dundee Grammar School and at St. Andrews
University (though born in Edinburgh of Aberdeenshire
parents), Fergusson was confident in his own classical
education, and could thus use Scots, when he needed to,
with a weight and a resonance that was denied to Ramsay
and Burns. It was altogether too late in the day for Ruddiman's Latin-based Scottish culture to take root; the two
significant cultural movements of eighteenth-century
Scotland were the antiquarian, nostalgic, revivalist
movement of collectors, editors, anthologists and anti-
quaries, which ran from Watson's *Choice Collection* to

Scott's *Minstrelsy of the Scottish Border* early in the next century and which was increasingly influenced by folk poetry and folk song, and the Scottish Enlightenment, which saw itself in the vanguard of progressive European thought. Fergusson hewed an independent line between the two, partly under the influence, conscious or not, of the Ruddiman-Freebairn tradition.

There were of course many permutations and combinations between these traditions. Walter Scott was to combine the antiquarian and folkloristic with the attitudes of the Scottish Enlightenment, and out of that combination came his creation of the historical novel. Many of the *literati*, men of the Enlightenment, defended Middle Scots as a great literary language on the lines laid down by Ruddiman and by Sir John Clerk of Penicuik (1676–1755) as (in Clerk's words) "genuine Saxon" in its purest form, full of "richness, energy and harmony" and sometimes went so far as to see it (as Clerk did) living on in its "native purity" in the spoken Scots of the common people. So there was encouragement from various quarters for any poet in the eighteenth century who wanted to try his hand at the revival of the vernacular for literary purposes, at least in poetry, in spite of the suspicion of Scots as, in David Hume's words, "a very corrupt dialect" of English and the desire by so many of the *literati* to purge their written works of "Scotticisms".

The complexity, if not the confusion, of the cultural situation is clearly shown in the works of Allan Ramsay (1684 or 1685–1758), who came to Edinburgh from his native Leadhills, Lanarkshire, at the turn of the century to become successively wig-maker, bookseller and man of letters. To the editorial function of Watson and Ruddiman he added that of reviser, populariser, experimenter, poet, *entrepreneur*, clubman, satirist, general busybody and spokesman for Scotland before the Queen Anne wits. He was not a scholar like Ruddiman, nor did he have Fergusson's education, but he was a great seeker

after knowledge and self-improvement. In 1712 he joined
with other young men in Edinburgh in founding the Easy
Club "in order that by a Mutual improvement in Conversation they may become more adapted for fellowship with
the politer part of mankind and Learn also from one
another's happy observations". The members of this club
all had pseudonyms, and Ramsay's was first Isaac Bicker-
staff (a fictitious person invented by Swift and taken up by
other Queen Anne writers) and later Gavin Douglas, thus
showing his dual interest in the Queen Anne wits and in
older Scottish literature. The Easy Club encouraged
Ramsay's gift for "occasional" poetry and also provided a
background of patriotic sentiment against which his
Scottish nationalism flourished vigorously. Isaac Bicker-
staff and Gavin Douglas; a gentleman of the Augustan
Age and an ardent Scottish patriot; an admirer of Pope
and Gay and Matthew Prior and a devoted champion of
the older Scottish Makars and of the use of vernacular
Scots by contemporary Scottish poets; a seeker after
polish and good breeding and a vulgar little gossip whose
schoolboy snigger spoils many of his poems and songs; a
sentimental Jacobite and a prudent citizen who cannily
absented himself from Edinburgh when Prince Charlie
held court in Holyrood in 1745; a champion of Scottish
folk song and a wrecker of scores of such songs by turning
them into stilted would-be neo-classic effusions—the
dualism in Ramsay's life and character was deep-seated
and reflected some of the confusions in the Scottish culture
of his day. He could defend the coarsest and frankest
language in poetry and yet dress up a Scottish song in
intolerable false elegancies. At the same time he could
demonstrate that he possessed the Horatian elegance of
the English gentleman by rendering an ode of Horace in
vivid and homely Scots verse.

In 1718 Ramsay first showed his interest in older
Scottish literature by bringing out, anonymously in
broadsides, several editions of "Christis Kirk on the

Grene" (with the same stanza form as Watson had used, different from the text he was to use in his anthology of older Scottish poetry, *The Ever Green*, in 1724). In the same year he also brought out his Elegies on Maggy Johnston, John Cowper and Lucky Wood in which he displayed his best vernacular vein. These poems are in the tradition that Ramsay himself, in a verse epistle to Hamilton of Gilbertfield, called "Standart *Habby*", the tradition of comic elegy popularised by Robert Sempill. The Elegy on Lucky Wood laments the loss of an honest and hospitable alehouse keeper in the Canongate, moving from elegy to reminiscent conviviality. There is a fine sense of atmosphere in the poem, with the scenes etched in warm and lively colours like a Breughel painting of a village celebration. Ramsay could do this sort of thing well, using an urban vernacular Scots that has no classical underpinning like Fergusson's but has considerable vitality. Ramsay used a different kind of Scots in his pastoral poetry, notably in his verse play *The Gentle Shepherd*, where his shepherds use a rustic Scots with a quiet formality that he does not readily manage elsewhere. Details of rural labour and rural festivity are handled with observant precision, and though there are some melodramatic moments connected with the return of the Royalist laird Sir William Worthy there is an atmosphere of country work and play pervading the whole which the pastoral had long lost in England and elsewhere in Europe. Altogether this pastoral drama represents a precarious equilibrium for Ramsay; in it he found a way of combining vernacular realism and a rather tired convention without incongruity or vulgarity.

Ramsay's most original work in Scots is his poems of Edinburgh low life and those of his songs (such as "My Peggy is a young thing", which is really as much English as Scots) where he does not destroy an older folk poem by impossible genteelisms. He experimented in older Scottish meters other than "Standart *Habby*": in "The

Poet's Wish" he uses "The Cherrie and the Slae" stanza for exactly the same purpose as Burns was to use it in his "Epistle to Davie" (which is based in many respects on Ramsay's poem and actually quotes a line from it). But more important than Ramsay's original work (which includes thirty-one fables and tales in fast-moving octosyllabic couplets and a lively Scots idiom) was his work as an editor. In *The Tea-Table Miscellany* (1724) he collected songs and ballads (both original, "improved" and imitated) and in *The Ever Green* he printed work of the Makars from the Bannatyne Manuscript. His intention in both collections was patriotic, as was Watson's. He makes this intention clear in his preface to *The Ever Green*:

> When these good old *Bards* wrote, we had not yet made Use of imported Trimming upon our Cloaths, nor of foreign Embroidery in our Writings. Their *Poetry* is the Product of their own Country, not pilfered and spoiled in the Transportation from abroad; Their *Images* are native, and their *Landskips* domestick; copied from those Fields and Meadows we every Day behold.

Here Ramsay's patriotism has obscured the fact that in reality the great Scottish Makars had the freedom of all European literature and borrowed confidently where they found anything useful to their art and craft. It is a measure of the defensive narrowness of much Scottish feeling after the Union that Ramsay should consider it a matter of praise that (as he wrongly believed) earlier Scottish poets should have had no truck with poets of other languages and countries. Fergusson's feelings about the invasion of Scots music by Italian influences has something in common with this, though it had more justification in fact.

The Ever Green had nothing like the popularity of *The Tea-Table Miscellany*. There were no reprints of it in Ramsay's lifetime, and four later reprints between 1761 and 1876. It was the popular vernacular tradition and the tradition of the late sixteenth-century poets that were available to Fergusson and Burns; the fifteenth-century Makars had no direct influence on eighteenth-century Scottish poetry. The relatively homogeneous national culture of the Lowland Scotland of the early Stewarts was too far away; 1560, 1603 and 1707 and all that those dates implied had between them created too wide a gulf between past and present, and complicated the Scottish cultural situation to the point where no real contact could any longer be made with Henryson and Dunbar. Much imitation folk song continued to be written, but in the years immediately after Ramsay's death there was no strong line of Scottish poetry discernible. When Fergusson came on the scene he had to make his own assessment and his own choice.

NOTE

1. Helena Mennie Shire, *Song, Dance and Poetry of the Court of Scotland Under King James VI*, Cambridge, 1969, p. 11.

CHAPTER II

Fergusson was born in Edinburgh on 5 September 1750 in the Cap-and-Feather Close, one of the alleys entering the High Street from the north that disappeared when the North Bridge was constructed. His parents had come to the city from Aberdeenshire some two years earlier. His father William Fergusson was a man of some education and ability, and he appears to have known better days in Tarland, Aberdeenshire, before apparently some kind of loss or failure induced him to settle in Edinburgh, where he managed to earn a not very lavish income in a succession of clerking jobs. His wife, Elizabeth Forbes, came from a fairly well off landed family in the parish of Kildrummie. Before they left Tarland the Fergussons had a son Hary, born in 1742, a daughter Barbara, born in 1744, and a son John (who apparently died in infancy) in 1746. A second daughter, Margaret, was born in Edinburgh in 1753. Robert Fergusson was the first child born in Edinburgh, and the second youngest.

There is a tradition that William Fergusson had some literary talent. Thomas Ruddiman (son of the Thomas Ruddiman discussed earlier and cousin of the founder and editor of *The Weekly Magazine* which first published Robert Fergusson's poems), who knew the family, recorded that William Fergusson "had also a turn to poetry, which he exercised in little satirical rhymes on occasional subjects, though his natural modesty and good disposition never allowed him to run into malicious personality".[1] According to A. B. Grosart, whose edition of Fergusson's poems includes a biography based on early manuscript material that has since disappeared, William Fergusson's "whole yearly income was hardly £20, and when not less than five individuals were wholly dependent on his exertions, we find that £1 15s. was spared for 'school payments,' a fact which cannot receive too much prominence".[2] Robert's mother taught him to read and in 1757, when he was in his seventh year, he was sent to a private school in Niddry's Wynd run by a Mr. Philp. He remained with Mr. Philp for six months. It appears as a child he was often ill, which may account for his relatively late starting of formal schooling. Indeed, his nephew, James Inverarity, later recorded that "during the years of infancy and childhood, the constitution of our poet was so weak, that little hopes were entertained of his arriving at manhood".[3] However, he was well enough to enter the High School in 1758, and he is on record as having attended also in 1759 and 1761, ill health having apparently interrupted his attendance in 1760. At the High School he was a pupil of John Gilchrist, who had a reputation as a Latin scholar. The novelist and essayist Henry Mackenzie who was born in 1745, five years before Fergusson, left an account of the High School curriculum at the time:

> The scholars went through the four classes taught by under-masters, reading the usual elementary Latin books (for at that time no Greek was taught at the High School) and so up to Virgil and Horace, Sallust and parts of Cicero. They were then removed to the Rector's Class, where they read portions of Livy along with the other classics above mentioned.[4]

Robert, however, did not go on to the Rector's class, having been successful in obtaining a bursary to the Grammar School of Dundee in 1762. This was a "mortification" left by David Fergusson of Strathmartine, providing for the "maintenance and education of two poor male children" of his own surname at the Grammar

School of Dundee until the age of fourteen and later, if
considered worthy, for four years at the University of St.
Andrews. It was apparently the influence of John Forbes,
his mother's brother, which procured the bursary for
Robert. He entered St. Andrews University in December
1764.

Meanwhile, William Fergusson's financial circumstances had improved. In 1763 he became accountant or
managing-clerk in the Linen-Department of the British
Linen Company in the Canongate and remained in this
post until his death in 1767, "never having great emolu-
ments," as Grosart put it, "but being much less pushed".[5]
His daughter Barbara married David Inverarity in 1764:
their son James later handed down reminiscences of
Robert invaluable to later biographers. In 1764 or 1765
William Fergusson moved with his family to Warriston's
Close on the north side of the High Street opposite St.
Giles'.

After leaving Dundee Grammar School and before
entering St. Andrews University Fergusson spent August
1764 with his mother at the farm of his uncle John Forbes
at Roundlichnot, near Old Meldrum, Aberdeenshire. A
letter from Edinburgh to his wife at Roundlichnot, written
by William Fergusson on 17 August 1764 with
characteristic quiet affection and wit, expresses pleasure
"that Rob has held out the journey", which suggests that
his health was still not robust.[6] Robert's association with
Aberdeenshire was thus not merely through his parents:
he had personal experience of the north-east, and this,
combined with his experience of Dundee and St.
Andrews, gave a breadth to his awareness of spoken Scots
that he would never have acquired had he been bound to
Edinburgh all his life.

The Arts course at St. Andrews at the time required the
study of Latin and Greek in the first year with the addition
of Mathematics and Logic in the second year, of Moral
Philosophy and more advanced Mathematics in the third,

and of Natural Philosophy in the fourth. Thomas Ruddiman recorded that "Virgil and Horace were the only Latin authors he would ever look at while at the University". Grosart possessed Fergusson's college copy of Xenophon's *Anabasis* and noted: "While he has duly written, 'Ex libris Robt. Fergusson' on the fly-leaf underneath, his wayward pen has sketched a rude drawing of a harp." Though he seems to have lacked any great enthusiasm for classical studies, Grosart reports that "his classical attainments were respectable", but, strangely perhaps, he seemed to have excelled at mathematics; his nephew James Inverarity actually claimed that "he was confessedly the first mathematician of his standing".[7]

St. Andrews University was not a distinguished centre of learning in Fergusson's day. The Principal, Thomas Tullidelph, seems to have been a man of some character, respected and even feared by both students and professors, but the only professors of any reputation were Robert Watson, Professor of Rhetoric, and the eccentric William Wilkie of the Chair of Natural Philosophy. It was recorded by one who knew Wilkie that "he had never met with a man who approached so near the two extremes of a god and a brute". He enjoyed a reputation as a poet, but his ambitious Homeric work *The Epigoniad* (1757) is unreadable, even though it led David Hume to hail him as the Scottish Homer. Wilkie took a personal interest in Fergusson, and he used to take him on visits to his farm about four miles from St. Andrews, where he exercised his skills as agricultural improver. It was Wilkie who appears to have interceded with Principal Tullidelph to get Fergusson pardoned for a prank he played that gave offence to his teachers. The offence was recorded in Tullidelph's journal on 26 March 1768:

I extruded Alexander Grant sine spe redeundi [without hope of return] on account of a continued

Course of irregularity for some weeks past—
particularly for a Riot committed with some
accomplices on Lewis Grant about one o'clock in the
morning of this 26th March.

And also extruded Robt. Ferguson, and Charles
Stewart his accomplice in that Riot. Rot. Ferguson
likewise had wantonly given up John Adamson's name
to be prayed for . . ..

N.B.—30th March 1768, Rot. Ferguson and Charles
Stewart were received in again at a meeting of the
Masters.[8]

Dr. Charles Webster, who had been a fellow student of
Fergusson's later told Alexander Campbell what
Fergusson had actually done to John Adamson.

He was considered the best singer in the university, of
consequence, he was oftener than he inclined,
requested to officiate as clerk at morning and evening
prayers. In order to get quit of this drudgery, he medi-
tated the following scheme. It is usual, according to the
Scottish mode of Presbyterian worship, to mention the
names of persons, who are recommended in prayer; our
poet, who, as usual, was in the precentor's desk, rose up
with great composure, and with an audible voice, as if
reading from a paper he held in his hand, said
"Remember in prayer a young man (who was in the
hall at the very instant) who, from the sudden effects of
inebriety, there appears but small hope of recovery."
This, as might be expected, threw the whole students
into a sudden fit of laughter. The professors wist not
what to do, and the assembly broke up, and dismissed
in peals of convulsive merriment. The indecorous
behaviour had nearly cost young Fergusson his gown;
and had not Dr Wilkie (the ingenious author of the
Epigoniad) stept in between him and the displeasure of
the rest of the professors, it may easily be conjectured
what would have been the consequences.[9]

These stories give a vivid impression of Fergusson as a lively, humorous, even at times riotous student, and this is borne out by all the traditions about his university days that have come down. There are no further suggestions of physical weakness during this period. He seems to have had a full and happy social life. He sang, and he wrote poetry. David Gregory, who gave up the Chair of Mathematics at the end of the academic year 1763–4 and died on 13 April 1765, is the subject of one of Fergusson's earliest efforts in verse, significantly in Scots, and in the direct tradition of the mock elegy (yet Fergusson's poem is both serious and humorous) of "Habbie Simson". It first appeared in the 1773 volume of Fergusson's poems, though it must have been handed round among his fellow students at the university. The poem is entitled "Elegy, on the Death of Mr David Gregory, late Professor of Mathematics in the University of St Andrews". It both perpetuates and extends an old tradition of Scots verse, being closely modelled on Robert Sempill's "Epitaph on Sanny Briggs" and William Hamilton of Gilbertfield's "Last Dying Words of Bonny Heck, a Famous Grey-Hound in the Shire of Fife" (both poems are in Watson's *Choice Collection*) and including also an echo of Ramsay's "Elegy on Maggy Johnston", but at the same time it is original, as Matthew McDiarmid has pointed out, in being the first poem in this tradition to have a "respectable" person as a subject.[10] Habbie Simson was a piper, Sanny Briggs was "nephew to Habbie Simpson, and Butler to the Laird of Kilbarchan" (as subtitled in Watson), Bonny Heck was a greyhound and Maggy Johnston was an ale-wife.

The opening of Fergusson's poem can be compared with the first stanza of the "Epitaph on Sanny Briggs". Here is Fergusson:

> Now mourn, ye college masters a'!
> And frae your ein a tear lat fa',

> Fam'd *Gregory* death has taen awa'
> remedy   Without remeid;
> The skaith ye've met wi's nae that sma',
>   Sin Gregory's dead.

And here is the opening stanza of "Sanny Briggs" as printed by Watson:

> Alake for evermore and wae!
> thirsty   To wha shall I whan drouthie gae?
> sorrow; trouble Dool, Sturt and Sorrow will me slae
>   without remeid,
>   For Hardship; and alake a day!
>   since *Sanny's* dead.

The phrase "without remeid" (originally a legal term, without "remeid of law" or appeal to a higher court) had become traditional in this kind of poem. It is found in "The Last Dying Words of Bonny Heck":

> Alas, alas, qho'bonny *Heck*,
> On former Days when I reflect!
> I was a Dog much in Respect
>   For doughty Deeds:
> But now I must hing by the Neck
>   Without Remeed.

The phrase is also found in the thirteenth stanza of Ramsay's "Elegy on Maggy Johnston":

> But now since 'tis sae that we must
> Not in the best ale put our trust,
> But whan we're auld return to dust
>   Without remead,
> Why should we tak it in disgust
>   That Maggy's dead?

In two of these cases "remeid" rhymes with "dead" (pronounced "deed"), as it does also in Fergusson. To that extent Fergusson's idiom is conventional and even mechanical. But his poem is different. The thirsty speaker who bewails the death of Sanny Briggs because he will now have nowhere to go to slake his thirst, the speaking greyhound who bewails his imminent hanging and the resigned mourner for Maggy Johnston who realises that even the drinkers of the best ale will one day turn to dust— these characters are all speaking with a conscious jocularity. The poems are *mock* elegies. Though a note of sly humour emerges in Fergusson's poem, it is not a mock elegy. He can refer to Gregory's mastery of Newton's theory of fluxions with an amused light-hearted literalness:

> He could, by *Euclid*, prove lang sine
> A ganging *point* compos'd a line;   moving
> By numbers too he cou'd divine,
>   Whan he did read,
> That *three* times *three* just made up nine;
>   But now he's dead.

The last four lines here are definitely reductive and indeed almost mocking, yet the tone never moves into pure mockery. He was skilled in algebra, too, the poem goes on to say:

> He cou'd make clear baith B's and A's
>   Wi' his lang head;
> Rin owr surd roots, but cracks or   run over; without
>   flaws;
>   But now he's dead.

A comic note emerges in the rhymes:

> Weel vers'd was he in architecture,
> An' kent the nature o' the *sector*,
> Upon baith globes he weel cou'd lecture
>   An' gar's tak heid;
> Of Geometry he was the *hector*;
>   But now he's dead.

Yet the comic tone is controlled; Gregory remains a

serious subject in spite of the humour that intervenes; the suggestion is of the kind of affectionate reminiscence of the dead one might get at a wake. The conclusion touches on a more serious elegiac tradition—comfort from the thought of the ultimate resurrection of the dead man—with a lightness that is not mockery:

> Great 'casion hae we a' to weep,
>
> An' cleed our skins in mourning deep,
>
> For Gregory *death* will fairly keep
>
> > To take his nap;
>
> He'll till the resurrection sleep
>
> > As sound's a tap.

clothe

The final phrase "as sound's a tap" is found in a very different context in Ramsay's "Maggy Johnston"

drunk

ridges

strip of untilled land

sought; lullaby

> Ae simmer nicht I was sae fou,
>
> Amang the riggs I geed to spew;
>
> Syne down on a green bank, I trow
>
> > I took a nap
>
> And soucht a' night balililow
>
> > As sound's a tap.

Fergusson has both Ramsay's phrase and his rhyming of "tap" with "nap", yet the difference between a drunkard's stupified sleep and the sleep of the just until the resurrection is enormous. Fergusson is delicately trying to steer a tradition of pure comic vulgarity into something rather more weighty. This early poem of his is not a masterpiece, certainly, but it shows Fergusson's concern with *tone*, his interest in moving easily between the grave and the gay, his desire to mediate between a rollicking vulgar vernacular Scots and something more quietly serious. It would be too much to say that this counterpointing of tones is wholly successful; but the attempt is there, and it is important.

No other poem of Fergusson's student days has survived. He is said to have gathered material for a tragedy on the death of Sir William Wallace during his period at St. Andrews and to have completed two acts before abandoning the project on discovering that another play (probably Gabriel Nisbet's *Caledon's Tears: Or Wallace—A Tragedy*) had been published on this subject and he did not want to be considered an imitator. The subject indicates his strong patriotic Scottish feeling, which was to be reflected in other ways as well. In the tradition of the north-east where his parents came from and of the elder Thomas Ruddiman, he had Jacobite sympathies, these being less a conviction that the House of Stewart ought to return to the throne than a feeling, not uncommon among certain sections of Scots from Watson and Ramsay to his own day and loosely associated with Jacobitism, that the Union of 1707 was a disaster for Scotland's nationhood and led to the overwhelming of Scottish identity by English interests. As we shall see, this was to be a significant theme in his poem "The Ghaists: a Kirk-yard Eclogue" (May 1733):

> Black be the day that e'er to
>   England's ground
> Scotland was eikit by the UNION's   enlarged
>   bond.

Fergusson left St. Andrews in May 1768 without taking a degree, which did not imply failure in any sense because the conferring of degrees at St. Andrews had become relatively uncommon at this time and many students left without this formality. His father had died in May 1767. The Fergusson family, impoverished by the death of the bread-winner, moved to poorer quarters in Jamieson's Land, Bell's Wynd, just east of Parliament Close. Robert's elder brother Hary had been driven by what he himself called in a letter to Robert "my past follies" (presumably his debts) to join the Navy. Robert was needed at home to help support his mother and his younger sister Margaret. He is said to have been urged to

study for the ministry, or to take up medicine or law, but
in the circumstances none of these was possible: he needed
a job right away, and in any case his sceptical habit of
mind on religious matters made the ministry quite
inappropriate, while he felt himself wholly unable to
endure the life of a doctor involving constant association
with scenes of disease and death. It seems clear that his
main interest was already writing poetry, and that he
wished for some rather undemanding job that would
enable him to support himself, his mother and sister while
allowing him to cultivate the literary life.

Before looking for a position in Edinburgh he made an
effort to secure help from his maternal uncle, John Forbes,
and visited his farm in Roundlichnot, near Old Meldrum.
He spent six months there, and in the end came away hurt
and indignant. The tradition of what happened that came
down from Fergusson's own family is preserved in David
Irving's account in his *Lives of the Poets* (vol. II, 1804) and
his earlier *Life of Fergusson* (1799). Forbes grew
increasingly embarrassed at his nephew's growing shab-
biness and after six months dismissed him from his house.
"Filled with indignation at the unworthy treatment which
he had received, he retired to a little solitary inn that stood
at a small distance; and having procured pen, ink, and
paper, wrote a letter to his unfeeling relation, couched in
terms of manly resentment. After his departure, Mr.
Forbes seems to have relented; he despatched a messenger
to him with a few shillings, to bear his expenses on the
road. This paltry present, the lowness of his funds com-
pelled him to accept. He set out for Edinburgh on foot,
and with much difficulty reached his mother's house."[11]
John Forbes's grandson rejected this account, explaining
that Fergusson appeared at the dinner table when two
wealthy and influential guests were present straight from
a wild country ramble in which he had dirtied and torn his
best clothes, at which John Forbes showed his irritation
by ordering him to leave the room, but soon afterwards,

hearing that he had left on the Aberdeen road and realising that he must have hurt the sensitive young man's feelings, sent a messenger after him on horseback with an apologetic letter and an entreaty to return, or, if not, at least to accept money to provide for his journey back to Edinburgh, but Fergusson refused to return and rejected the offer of money.[12]

So, whichever version of the events we accept, it is clear that Fergusson returned home with no further hope of help through his uncle's influence. Shortly afterwards he obtained a position as clerk or copyist in the Commissionary Office at the rate of a penny per page transcribed. It was mechanical and ill-paid work, but it provided him with sufficient to enable him to develop his contacts with musical and theatrical circles as well as his talents as a poet. He wrote poetry, he sang songs, and he made friends.

In January 1769 an opera called *The Royal Shepherd*, with music by George Rushe and libretto by Richard Rolt was performed at the Theatre Royal, Edinburgh. (This theatre was built in the Canongate in 1746–7, in spite of clerical opposition, and it was here that John Home's *Douglas* was performed in 1756. Soon afterwards it was destroyed in a riot, but was re-opened in 1767 with a play to which the young James Boswell wrote a prologue. After December 1769, when the New Theatre was opened where the General Post Office now stands, it fell into disrepair, hence Fergusson's "burlesque poem", entitled "The Canongate Play-House in Ruins", written in July 1772). *The Royal Shepherd* contained "alterations" in the form of fourteen extra or altered songs which, though they never appeared with Fergusson's name, we now know to have been almost certainly written by him. They are in the conventional English poetic idiom of the time and are quite undistinguished. But they show that Fergusson was moving in literary and musical circles.

The principal role in *The Royal Shepherd* was sung by the

popular Italian singer Giusto Ferdinando Tenducci, who was much admired in Edinburgh and became a good friend of Fergusson's. Tenducci returned to Edinburgh in May 1769 to fulfil a contract with the Musical Society. On 29 July 1769, at a concert at the Theatre Royal for his benefit, Tenducci sang the role of Arbaces in Thomas Arne's popular opera *Artaxerxes*. To this performance Fergusson contributed three songs set to traditional Scottish airs, "Braes of Bellenden", "Roslin Castle" and "Lochaber No More", sung by Tenducci to the great applause of the audience. They use a rather stilted and even pretentious English diction ("By Heav'n's displeasure the wretch thus is thrown,/With tempests harsh sounding on seas yet unknown", or "What doubts oppress my wounded heart!/My soul at every breath doth start!"), although the third song, to the tune "Lochaber No More", does at least move with some fluency:

> O where shall I wander my lover to find,
> And with sweet discourses indulge my fond mind?
> . . .

But a poet who can write "with sweet discourses" has not yet found his proper idiom.

Tenducci left Edinburgh about the middle of November, but never forgot his relationship with Fergusson, whom he remembered with tears when talking to the poet Campbell long after Fergusson's death. Fergusson made other musical friends in Edinburgh. They included the composer, song-writer and singer Cornforth Gilson, the singer John Smeaton, the Musical Society's conductor Ferdinand Arrigoni, Stephen Clarke, who was to help Burns in transcribing airs for his songs, and the composer John Collet, who set to music Fergusson's ode (in neo-classic English) on "The Rivers of Scotland". Fergusson was also passionately fond of the theatre and made friends with actors. He would most probably have attended the performance of Steele's

Conscious Lovers at the opening of the New Theatre on 7 December 1769. He made friends with West Digges, the actor who took over the management of the New Theatre in 1771 and his leading actor William Woods. Woods obtained free admission to the theatre for Fergusson, and he attended regularly. Robert Chambers handed down a memory of his behaviour at the theatre: "He always sat in the central box, denominated the Shakespeare box; and his mode of expressing approbation in comic perfor-mances was very singular. Instead of clapping his hands, or using any exclamations, he used to show how much he was delighted by raising his right hand clenched above his head, and bringing it down emphatically on the front of the box, with a sweeping blow."[13]

Another friend of Fergusson's at this period was Robert Anderson, a medical student and theatre lover, later the editor of *British Poets*. They first met "at one Stuart's (a bookseller's shop in Candle-maker-row) in 1771" and used to frequent the theatre together. It was his theatrical interests that brought Fergusson membership of the Robinhood Society, which he refers to in his poem "Mutual Complaint of Plainstanes and Causey" and explains the reference with a note indicating it as "a new instituted society, held weekly in the Thistle Lodge, where the grand concerns of the nation are debated by a set of juvenile Cicero's". It later changed its name to the Pan-theon.

More important for Fergusson's social life than the Robinhood Society was the Cape Club, one of the many Edinburgh clubs of the period, less socially and intellectually pretentious than the Select Society and the Poker Club where members of the *literati* met to discuss philosophical and general questions. The Cape Club was formally founded in 1764, having existed informally since 1733, and survived until 1841. David Herd prefaced the Club's *sederunt* book with an account of its purpose and activities: "The purpose and intention of the Society from the beginning was: after the business of the day was over to pass the evening socially with a set of select companions in an agreeable but at the same time a rational and frugal manner; for this purpose beer or porter were their liquors, from fourpence to sixpence each the extent of their usual expence, conversation and a song their amusement, gaming generally prohibited, and a freedom for each to come and depart at their pleasure was always considered as essential to the constitution of the Society." Members were united by a sense of community which drew no social or professional lines at all. Each member assumed a knightly title. In Fergusson's time members included David Herd himself (Sir Scrape); Thomas Lancashire the actor (Sir Cape); Alexander Runciman the painter (Sir Brimstone); Sir James Cummyng (Sir Nun and Abbess), lyon clerk, heraldic painter and later secretary of the Antiquarian Society; and John Witherspoon, Herd's collaborator and printer. It was perhaps the most democratic of all the Edinburgh societies of the period. Hans Hecht, in his edition of *Songs from David Herd's Manuscripts* (1904), examined all the surviving records of the Club and has given the fullest account of it:

> The guild of writers [lawyers] sent many members, but tradesmen were in the great majority: shoemakers, tailors, glovemakers, smiths, saddlers, marble-cutters, barbers, brewers were admitted; and that the masters were not void of the necessary humour appears from many a merry document now hidden in the solemn volumes of the club. With them sat a few advocates, writers to the signet, surgeons and doctors, ship-owners and naval officers; even a solitary student of divinity appears in the lists. A bohemian element was not wanting to give its peculiar share to the merriment. With Alexander Runciman came painters, such as John Brown, Jacob More, Alexander Nasmyth, Sir Henry Raeburn; musicians, who played no small part

at the meetings, as Stephen Clarke, the collaborator of
James Johnson and Burns in the *Musical Museum*, the
German F. G. C. Schetky, an Edinburgh celebrity, . . .
and the great song-reciter James Balfour, whose skill in
rendering Scotch songs must have been incomparable.
The stage was represented by actors, like Thomas
Lancashire and William Woods . . . and by William
Kemble, manager to the Theatre Royal. We may add
the names of some other well-known personalities:
James Sibbald, the compiler of the *Chronicle of Scottish
Poetry*, Robert Fergusson's biographer . . . Even the
elegant and ingenious William Brodie was of the
company. He was hanged on October 1st, 1788, on a
gibbet of his own construction, for putting the finishing
touches to a long series of burglaries by robbing the
excise-office.[14]

Fergusson appears to have made David Herd's
acquaintance in 1769, and to have been introduced by him
and other friends to the Cape Club, to which he was
formally admitted a member in October 1772, sponsored
by Herd and James Cummyng. He assumed the title of Sir
Precentor, because of his good singing voice and perhaps
also with reference to the St. Andrews episode already
described. The Club met in various Edinburgh taverns,
most often, in Fergusson's day, at Walter Scott's in
Geddes Close, on the north side of the High Street. It had
elaborate statutes and a number of office-bearers with
grandiose titles (the Sovereign being the chief). Poetry
and music as well as conviviality were their interests, and
they celebrated the memory of poets of the past in particular festivities (thus the sixth Grand Cape was held on 6
September 1769 in "honour of the immortal memory of
William Shakespeare" and on 22 September of the same
year they celebrated James Thomson's birthday with a
"general festival".)
    The Cape Club provided a better atmosphere for a poet

than the self-conscious young would-be gentlemen of the
Easy Club had provided for Ramsay. Fergusson was at
home there, as he was at home "o'er oysters and a dram o'
gin" at Lucky Middlemass's tavern or with a dish of
rizzard haddock and a bicker of tippenny at this or some
other Edinburgh howff. He celebrated the Cape in his
finest Edinburgh poem, "Auld Reikie":

> But chief, O *Cape*! we crave thy aid
poverty
> To get our cares and poortith laid:
> Sincerity, and genius true,
> Of knights have ever been the due:
> Mirth, music, porter deepest dy'd,
> Are never here to worth deny'd;
> And health, o' happiness the queen,
shines
> Blinks bonny, wi' her smile serene.

A great deal of excessive drinking and riotous behaviour
went on in the evenings in Edinburgh's taverns and streets
in Fergusson's day, as the poet records in his poems about
the city, and doubtless Fergusson had his occasions of
excess. But the Cape Club did not indulge in the riotous
behaviour of some of the more advanced Edinburgh clubs,
nor did its members emulate the practice of many
eminent judges and advocates who, sitting at home over
their claret or port, went nightly drunk to bed. The range
of convivial pastimes was considerable. Oyster cellars,
"laigh shops" and taverns of varying degrees of comfort or
squalor were scenes of nightly gatherings. Robert
Chambers, in the chapter of his *Traditions of Edinburgh*
entitled "Conviviala", records with an air of surprised
disapproval some of the convivialities, in which ladies
indulged as well as gentlemen. "In winter, when the
evening had set in, a party of the most fashionable people
in town, collected by appointment, would adjourn in
carriages to one of those abysses of darkness and comfort,
called, in Edinburgh, *laigh shops*, where they proceeded to
regale themselves with raw oysters and porter [the Forth

at that time was still famous for its oysters], arranged in huge dishes upon a coarse table, in a dingy room, lighted by tallow candles."[15] Chambers contrasted early nineteenth-century Edinburgh society with that of the late eighteenth century, when "the characteristic sobriety of the nation's manners was only traceable in certain portions of society". Boswell records some startling excesses in his journals, and though he was not altogether typical he was certainly not in this respect a remarkable exception.

Soon after Fergusson's early death in 1774 the tradition became established (as it did in the case of Burns also) that he died young because of his dissolute life. "Fergusson, dissipated and drunken, died in early life, after having produced poems faithfully and humorously describing scenes in Edinburgh of festivity and somewhat of blackguardism."[16] So wrote Henry Mackenzie (born in 1745) in his old age. He added, for good measure, that Burns's "admiration of Fergusson showed his propensity to coarse dissipation". Such traditions die hard. Even A. B. Grosart, in the sympathetic biography prefixed to his edition of the poems, refers to the "crapulent habits of the whole society of Edinburgh at this period" and says that Fergusson "took refuge from his heart-breaking want, his unending drudgery, as 'a stricken deer singled out from the herd,' in the excitement and revelry of such scenes". He had information from the aged Miss Ruddiman, sister of the editor of *The Weekly Magazine*: "His 'cheek,' said Miss Ruddiman, "I have often heard my brother say, would 'redden' through its paleness if but a hint of such 'meetings' was thrown out: and once on being reproved, he said, with the tears bursting from between his fingers as he held them over his face, 'Oh! Sir, anything to forget my poor mother and these aching fingers'."[17] Such picturesque anecdotes are suspect. Nineteenth-century clergymen looking back on the habits of eighteenth-century Edinburgh poets do not provide the most reliable evidence.

The records of the Cape Club are more trustworthy. But
the best evidence is that provided by the poems
themselves.

NOTES

1. A. B. Grosart, ed. *The Works of Robert Fergusson; with Life of the Author
   and an Essay on His Genius and Writings*, London, Edinburgh, and
   Dublin, 1879, p. xxviii.
2. *Ibid.*, p. xxxvi.
3. George Gleig, *Supplement to the Third Edition of the Encyclopedia
   Britannica*, I, Edinburgh, 1801, p. 647. Gleig got his information from
   James Inverarity, so his account has some authority.
4. Harold William Thompson, ed., *The Anecdotes and Egotisms of Henry
   Mackenzie 1745–1831*, London, 1927, p. 34.
5. Grosart, *op. cit.*, p. xlvii.
6. *Ibid.*, p. xlv.
7. Gleig, *op. cit.*, p. 647.
8. Matthew P. McDiarmid, ed., *The Poems of Robert Fergusson*, Scottish
   Text Society, Edinburgh and London, I, 1954, p. 17.
9. *Ibid.*, p. 18.
10. *Ibid.*, II, 1956, p. 248.
11. David Irving, *The Lives of the Scottish Poets*, Edinburgh, 1804, p. 418.
12. Grosart, *op cit.*, p. lxix.
13. Robert Chambers, *A Biographical Dictionary of Eminent Scotsmen*,
    Glasgow, 1835, II, p. 306.
14. Hans Hecht, ed., *Songs from David Herd's Manuscripts*, Edinburgh,
    1904, pp. 38-9.
15. *Select Writings of Robert Chambers*, VI, *Traditions of Edinburgh*, Edin-
    burgh, 1847, p. 140.
16. Henry Mackenzie ed. Thompson, *op. cit.*, p. 150.
17. Grosart, *op. cit.*, lxxxiii.

CHAPTER III

On 7 February 1771 *The Weekly Magazine* printed anonymously the first of three pastoral poems, entitled
respectively "Morning", "Noon" and "Night". The latter
two appeared in the issues of the 14th and 21st, and they
were all anonymous. But the first had an introductory
note by Walter Ruddiman: "We have been favoured with
three Pastorals, under the titles of Morning, Noon and
Night, written by a young Gentleman of this place, the
stile of which appears as natural and picturesque as that of
any of the modern ones hitherto published." The young
gentleman was Fergusson, and the poems are written in a
somewhat vapid style imitative of a strain of
English pastoral poetry that flourished in the eighteenth
century and was well represented by William Shenstone,
though Shenstone's pastoral poetry was more varied both
metrically and in mood than these efforts of Fergusson's.
(It is unfair to Shenstone to say, as Fergusson's editor
Matthew McDiarmid says in his preface, that the poems
are "just as tinkling and as amiably vapid as those of their
models, the pastorals of William Shenstone".[1] It is true
that Shenstone could be sententious and pretentious, as
sometimes in his posthumously published *Elegies*, which
certainly influenced Fergusson, but he was a genuine con-
noisseur of country scenery and of landscape; he had a gift
for epigram as well as meditative description, and he
could display a kind of mocking humour.) Fergusson's
first Pastoral, "Morning", is a dialogue between two
shepherds, Alexis and Damon. Alexis begins in
highly stylised verse:

> 'Tis thine to sing the graces of the morn,
> The zephyr trembling o'er the ripening corn:
> 'Tis thine with ease to chant the rural lay,
> While bubbling fountains to your numbers play . . ..

This is pretty mechanical stuff, written in a dead or dying tradition. But it is interesting that in his highly stylised language, put into the mouths of shepherds with names from Greek pastoral poetry, Fergusson introduces a familiar Edinburgh landscape:

> Behold Edina's lofty turrets rise,
> Her structures fair adorn the eastern skies;
> As Pentland cliffs o'er top yon distant plain,
> So she the cities on our north domain.

So we have Edinburgh, classicised into "Edina", and the Pentland Hills, as well as invocations to Ceres, Pan and Apollo and an abstract vocabulary of invocation of natural objects that trembles on the absurd:

> Ye balmy breezes, wave the verdant field,
> Clouds all your bounties, all your moisture yield; . . .

This is reminiscent of W. S. Gilbert's poem where the speaker addresses the world and tells it to roll on, and a concluding direction adds, "It rolls". The second Pastoral, "Noon", is in a similar style; it is a dialogue between the shepherds Corydon and Timanthes set at the time of day when "the sun the summit of his orb hath gained". The only flash of interest in the poem is the reference to the conflict between Lord North's government and "Wilkes and Liberty". Fergusson was a Scottish nationalist Tory (the phrase will become clearer later) and was very conscious of Wilkes's anti-Scottish attitude. Corydon laments that his love Delia is now in England, wandering "o'er the *Anglian* plain",

Where civil discord and sedition reign.
There Scotia's sons in odious light appear,
Tho' we for them have wav'd the hostile spear:
For them my sire, enwrapp'd in curdled gore,
Breath'd his last moments on a foreign shore.

The sentiment—protest against anti-Scottish attitudes in England in spite of the fact that Scots had died in England's imperialist wars—is more interesting than the language. But it is of some interest to note "Edina" and "Scotia"—Burns was to use both these terms with conspicuous lack of success—as attempts by Fergusson to classicise aspects of Scotland. He was to show the benefits of a classical education in more effective ways in some of his Scots poems. The third Pastoral, "Night", is characterised by a graver sententiousness and more edifying sentiments as Amyntas and Florellus moralise in the dusk. The style is something of a jumble, beginning with an evening scene reminiscent of Gray's "Elegy" and ending with something a little more Elizabethan:

Now *owls* and *batts* infest the midnight scene,
Dire snakes, invenom'd twine along the green; . . .

Another pastoral poem, entitled "The Complaint", is written in the lilting rhythms of Shenstone's "Pastoral Ballad in Four Parts". It did not appear in *The Weekly Magazine* but in the volume of Fergusson's poems published in 1773. It has some biographical interest, for Damon is represented singing of his unrequited love for Stella, and Stella was a real person (she wrote a poem on Fergusson after his death) who married someone else but retained an interest in the poet. Shenstone's poem opens:

Ye shepherds give ear to my lay,
    And take no more heed to my sheep:
They have nothing to do but to stray;
    I have nothing to do but to weep.

Damon's lament, in Fergusson's poem, begins:

> O Cupid! thou wanton young boy!
>   Since, with thy invisible dart,
> Thou hast robb'd a fond youth of his joy,
>   In return grant the wish of his heart.

There is nothing in Fergusson's poem that could not have
been written by a minor English versifier of the period.
But it is interesting that Fergusson was attracted to this
metrical pattern, which is very like the metrical pattern of
some older Scots poems of popular revelry which he used
later in his "Hallow Fair". (We do not know the date of
"The Complaint", but it must have been composed some
time in 1772 at latest to have appeared in the 1773 volume.
"Hallow Fair" did not appear in Fergusson's lifetime, but
was communicated by him to David Herd, who printed it
in volume II of his *Scots Songs*, 1776. It was first attributed
to Fergusson in the index of James Johnson's *Scots Musical
Museum*, volume V, 1797.) Another of Fergusson's early
pastoral poems in the English Shenstonian mode is
"Written at the Hermitage of Braid, near Edinburgh",
which appeared in *The Weekly Magazine* on 10 October
1771. It has the same lilting metre, used by other eighteenth century English poets besides Shenstone, sometimes to suggest an almost ballad note. But there is
nothing of the ballad in Fergusson's poem:

> Would you relish a rural retreat,
>   Or the pleasure the groves can inspire?
> The city's allurements forget,
>   To this spot of enchantment retire . . ..

These early poetic essays of Fergusson are of no great
interest, but it is perhaps worth noting that although he
wrote them in a conventional English poetic diction he
clearly pronounced the words with a Scots accent. In
"Noon", for example, Corydon complains of his poverty,
since

> *Tay* bounding o'er *his* banks with awless sway,
> Bore all my corns—all my flocks away.

"Corns" is clearly disyllabic, with a long rolled "r".

"On the cold Month of April 1771", which appeared in *The Weekly Magazine* on 16 May 1771, is written in the style of Shenstone's *Elegies*, but at least it describes the real weather, having been provoked, apparently, by a poem entitled "April" that had appeared in the previous issue of the magazine giving a poetic account of spring weather as it is supposed to be and not as it was that year. Fergusson uses the unseasonable weather to moralise pretentiously about life:

> Life! What art thou? a variegated scene
>> Of mingl'd light and shade, of joy and woe;
> A sea where calms and storms promiscuous reign,
>> A stream where sweet and bitter jointly flow.

He goes on to describe how the plains are mute, the shepherd pipes no more, and winter still bestrides the blast, concluding with an appeal to Boreas to relent and allow spring to come. The language is almost ridiculously stylised, even when it tells the truth about the weather.

On 1 August 1771 a rather different sort of poem by Fergusson appeared in *The Weekly Magazine*. This was "A Saturday's Expedition. In Mock Heroics", written in the mock-Miltonic style popularised by John Philips' "The Splendid Shilling" and employed also, although with less comic intent if often with similar comic effect, in John Armstrong's "The Art of Preserving Health" and John Dyer's "The Fleece". This kind of style appealed to Fergusson's sense of humour, and he reverted to it more than once in the course of his short poetic career. The poem describes an expedition across the Forth to Fife, and Fergusson clearly relished the combination of a high-pitched epic style with local references:

> After regaling here with sober cann,
> Our limbs we plied, and nimbly measur'd o'er
> The hills, the vales, and the extensive plains,
> Which form the distance from *Burntisland*'s port
> To *Inverkeithing*. Westward still we went,
> Till in the ferry-boat we loll'd at ease;
> Nor did we long on Neptune's empire float,
> For scarce ten posting minutes were elaps'd
> Till we again on *Terra Firma* stood,
> And to M'Laren's march'd, where roasted lamb,
> With cooling lettuce, crown'd our social board.

Fergusson loved the Forth, and at one point in the poem he breaks out in its praise and sounds at the same time a characteristic Scottish patriotic note:

> Sweet navigable stream! where commerce reigns,
> Where peace and jocund plenty smile serene:
> On thy green banks sits Liberty enthron'd,
> But not that shadow which the English youth
> So eagerly pursue; but freedom bought
> When Caledonia's triumphant sword
> Taught the proud sons of Anglia to bemoan
> Their fate at *Bannockburn*, where thousands came
> Never to tread their native soil again.

A "pastoral elegy" in seventeen quatrains, entitled "The Decay of Friendship", appeared in *The Weekly Magazine* on 19 September 1771. It is a moralising poem in the style of Shenstone's *Elegies*, and still shows no sign of where Fergusson's real strength lay. Nor did his poem "A Burlesque Elegy on the amputation of a Student's Hair, before his Orders", which appeared on 21 November. This rather faint echo of "The Rape of the Lock" also owes something to Allan Ramsay's "On the most Honourable The Marquess of Bowmont's Cutting off his Hair". The poem concludes

Some skilful artist of a French *frizeur*,
   With graceful ringlets shall thy temples bind,
And cull the precious relics from the floor,
   Which yet may flutter in the wanton wind.

This does not really bear comparison with Pope's ending:

When those fair Suns shall set, as set they must,
And all those tresses shall be laid in dust;
This Lock, the Muse shall consecrate to Fame,
And midst the stars inscribe Belinda's name.

But then Fergusson was trying something much less ambitious.

None of the poems by Fergusson or indeed anybody else that had hitherto appeared in *The Weekly Magazine* could have prepared the readers for "The Daft Days" on 2 January 1772. At a stroke Fergusson now defined his position as a Scottish poet and an Edinburgh poet; he brought together his reading in English poetry, his knowledge of earlier Scots poetry and his classical education; he placed himself in a Scottish tradition that he revived and altered while drawing on it; he anchored the poem solidly in his own time and place while at the same time harking back to older styles and modes; and he created an enthusiastic audience for this kind of poetry without whom Burns would not have had the success he did have.

He did not, however, give up writing poems in Shenstonian and other English modes, but these, though sometimes showing a certain imitative skill, are so vapid in comparison with his Scots poems that the reader is not tempted to stay with them long. "Fashion. A Poem" appeared in *The Weekly Magazine* on 27 February 1772, and readers must have been bitterly disappointed when, instead of finding a successor to "The Daft Days", they read the opening:

> O Nature, parent goddess! at thy shrine,
> Prone to the earth, the muse, in humble song,
> Thy aid implores: . . .

But on 5 March they could read Fergusson's "Elegy on the Death of Scots Music". This is a belligerently nationalistic poem, yet it has as epigraph a quotation from Shakespeare's *Twelfth Night* that makes it clear that his interest is in the genuine, the native and the traditional rather than in Scottishness for its own sake:

> Mark it, Caesario; it is old and plain,
> The spinsters and the knitters in the sun,
> And the free maids that weave their thread with bones,
> Do use to chant it.

This sets the tone, and the poem (although it uses a traditional Scots stanza more associated with lively humour than with serious elegy) opens with an elegaic stateliness:

> On Scotia's plains in days of yore,
> When lads and lasses *tartan* wore,
> Saft Music rang on ilka shore,
> In hamely weid;
> But harmony is now no more,
> And *music* dead.

every
simple dress

"Scotia's plains" (rather than "Scotland's plains") gives evidence of a formality in the Scots language, and in its context the phrase comes off. Yet the formality is used to give weight to the subject rather than to distance it from the ordinary and the colloquial. Indeed, in some degree the subject is precisely regret at the disappearance of the ordinary and the colloquial, the loss of music that rang "in hamely weid" [dress]. And "weid" gives notice that "dead", though spelt in the conventional English manner, is to be pronounced as in Scots, "deid".

The next stanza employs the conventional neo-classic English phrase "feather'd choir" and the equally conventional "zephyrs", but accompanies them with the adverbs "bonnily" and "sleely" which domicile these phrases in a Scottish context. It is a remarkably bold combination, as is the use in the following stanza of "ilka nymph" and "ilka swain" (making "nymph" and "swain" into Scots words by prefixing "ilka") and the introduction of Naiads.

> Round her the feather'd choir would wing,
> Sae bonnily she wont to sing,
> And sleely wake the sleeping string,   skilfully
>   Their sang to lead,
> Sweet as the zephyrs of the spring;
>   But now she's dead.

> Mourn ilka nymph and ilka swain,   every
> Ilk sunny hill and dowie glen;   every; gloomy
> Let weeping streams and *Naiads* drain
>   Their fountain head;
> Let echo swell the dolefu' strain,
>   Since music's dead.

("Head" is presumably to be pronounced "heid" if "dead" is to be pronounced "deid", as it must be unless Fergusson intends to shift the pronunciation in this stanza. He might well be doing this, for although the word "dead" ends every stanza and in almost every other case is clearly to be pronounced "deid", in the eighth stanza he rhymes it with "stead" and, more definite indication, in the tenth he rhymes it with "bed". There is evidence in other poems, too, that Fergusson gave flexibility to his rhymes by adopting now an English and now a Scots pronunciation of a word.)

After four stanzas of lament in fairly general terms, Fergusson, in a manner characteristic of him, begins to narrow the subject with increasing particularisation (and

with an interesting suggestion of Jane Elliot's version of
"The Flowers o' the Forest"):

> Nae lasses now, on simmer days,
> Will lilt at bleaching of their claes;
> Nae herds on *Yarrow*'s bonny braes,
>   Or banks of *Tweed*,

home-bred
> Delight to chant their hameil lays,
>   Since music's dead.

> At glomin now the bagpipe's dumb,

oxen
> Whan weary owsen hameward come;

play
> Sae sweetly as it wont to bum,

lively playing
>   And *Pibrachs* skreed;
> We never hear its warlike hum;
>   For music's dead.

A reference to his favourite song, "The Birks of
Invermay", finishes the particularisation, and the poem
then moves at once to its formal conclusion:

once
> O SCOTLAND! that cou'd yence afford

overcome
> To bang the pith of Roman sword,
> Winna your sons, wi' joint accord,
>   To battle speed?
> And fight till MUSIC be restor'd,
>   Which now lies dead.

The poem shows an interesting combination of
influences and attitudes. The nostalgic Scottish
patriotism, that he found in some of Ramsay's poems, can
accommodate a reference to Shakespeare and an echo of
Gray ("What weary owsen hameward come"). Friend of
Tenducci though he was, he deplores the influence of
Italian music on the native Scots tradition. (It is quite true
that the Italianising of Scottish folk song went on
increasingly in the latter years of the eighteenth century
and can be seen in the excessive trills and ornaments in the
accompaniments in Thomson's *Select Scottish Airs*, but the

situation was more complex than that, and Fergusson's enthusiasm for his native tradition led him to over-simplify.) In one stanza he laments the death of Macgib-bon (or McGibbon):

> *Macgibbon*'s gane: Ah! waes my heart!
> The man in music maist expert,
> Wha cou'd sweet melody impart,
>   And tune the reed,
> Wi' sic a slee and pawky art;   skilful; cunning
>   But now he's dead.

The violinist and composer William McGibbon was born in Edinburgh about 1695 and died there in 1756. Though Fergusson contrasts McGibbon's native skills with imported Italian trash—

> Now foreign sonnets bear the gree,   prize
> And crabbit queer variety   perverse
> Of sounds fresh sprung frae *Italy*,
>   A bastard breed!
> Unlike that saft-tongu'd melody
>   Which now lies dead—

the fact is that McGibbon seems to have modelled his early career on Corelli, although after 1740 he became more and more interested in Scots fiddle music. Like Corelli, he made a name for himself both as a composer and as a violinist, and was Scotland's leading composer in the first half of the eighteenth century. Fergusson seems to have been less interested in his trio sonatas, his sonatas for flute and violin or two flutes and his other compositions in the Italian tradition of Corelli, and more interested in his settings of Scots folk tunes, of which he published one hundred and twenty-eight between 1742 and 1755. Yet even these combined, with remarkable success, the idiom of Scots folk music with the idiom of Italian baroque. Matthew McDiarmid has asserted that the idea of introducing McGibbon into the poem "though with a serious and not a comic purpose, certainly came from Hamilton of Gilbertfield's *The Life and Death of the Piper of Kilbarchan* and Ramsay's *Elegy on Patie Birnie*, 'the Famous Fiddler of Kinghorn'".[2] There is of course a continuous tradition working here, but the differences between the earlier poems and Fergusson's are more marked than the similarities. Fergusson's poem is about the dwindling integrity of Scottish culture, and it is part of his response to the fate of Scotland after the Union. The concluding apostrophe to Scotland (not, interestingly enough, to "Scotia") founded a special kind of rhetorical tradition in Scots poetry that Burns drew on in the conclusion of "The Cotter's Saturday Night".

On 7 May 1772 *The Weekly Magazine* published Fergusson's "Conscience. An Elegy", a rather feeble moralising poem in the Shenstonian tradition, but this was followed on 4 June by one of his finest pieces in Scots, "The King's Birth-Day in Edinburgh". This is a full-blooded performance in the Scottish tradition of poems of popular revelry though lacking what might be called the broadside accent of so many of such poems. It is a description of Edinburgh's celebration of George III's thirty-sixth birthday, of which an account was given in sober prose in *The Weekly Magazine* of 12 June, which describes both the official celebrations on the Castle Hill and in Parliament House and the rowdy activities of sections of the populace in the evening, when "the lower class of people" became "perfectly licentious" and "after their ammunition of squibs and crackers was exhausted, they employed dead cats, mud &c. which they discharged very plentifully on the city guard; and, when threatened to be chastised or apprehended, they betook themselves to the more dangerous weapons of stones and brickbats &c. In this encounter several of the guard were wounded, and they in return dealt their blows pretty liberally, by which, amid the confusion, some innocent persons suffered along with the guilty."

Fergusson's poem begins with an epigraph from that exuberant and very popular macaronic (or rather for the most part dog-Latin) poem by William Drummond of Hawthornden, "Polemo-Middinia", which appeared in the first volume of Watson's *Choice Collection* and was also included in a one-volume folio edition of Drummond's works in 1711. This kind of jocular use of the classics seems to have appealed to Fergusson from his student days: it is a taste that distinguished him sharply from both his predecessor Ramsay and his successor Burns, neither of whom was equipped by education, as Fergusson was, to relish this sort of student humour. The flavour of Drummond's poem can be judged from its opening lines:

> Nymphae, quae colitis highistima monta *Fifaea*,
> Seu vos *Pitenwema* tenent, seu *Crelia* crofta,
> Sive *Anstraea* domus, ubi nat *Haddocus* in undis,
> *Codlineusque* ingens, & *Fleucca* & *Sketa* pererrant
> Per costam, & scopulos, *Lobster* manifootus in udis
> Creepat, . . .

"Nymphs, who dwell in the highest mountain of Fife (presumably this is what Drummond means by "monta" which of course is not Latin unless it is a misprint for *monte*) whether you live in Pittenweem or the crofts of Crail or have your home in Anstruther, where the haddock swims in the waves, and the huge codling and the fluke and skate wander by the coast and the rocks, the many-footed lobster creeps in the wet, . . ." The combination of Latin, dog-Latin and Latinised Fife place names had a special appeal for Fergusson. But in fact, though his quotation from Drummond's poem reflects his knowledge of and interest in it, Fergusson is not here writing in this style at all. The epigraph consists of but one line from Drummond:

> *Oh! qualis hurly-burly fuit, si forte videsses.*

The poem then proceeds in a style that is familiar but not vulgar. The opening is humorous in a new way for eighteenth-century Scottish poetry:

	I sing the day sae aften sung,
ears	Wi' which our lugs hae yearly rung,
poured forth	In whase loud praise the Muse has dung
	A' kind o'print;
wench; baffled	But wow! the limmer's fairly flung;
	There's naething in't.. . .

trouble	O *Muse*, be kind, and dinna fash us
	To flee awa' beyont Parnassus,
	Nor seek for *Helicon* to wash us,
	That heath'nish spring;
throats	Wi' Highland whisky scour our hawses,
cause us to	And gar us sing.

	Begin then, dame, ye've drunk your fill,
	You wouldna hae the tither gill?
	You'll trust me, mair wou'd do you ill,
drive you crazy	And ding you doitet;
	Troth 'twou'd be sair agains my will
blame	To hae the wyte o't.

To rhyme the Scots phrase "dinna fash us" ("don't bother us") with "Parnassus" shows a certain boldness in claiming the right to use classical references in a rollicking Scots poem, and this is what Fergusson must have learned, directly or indirectly, from the tradition of vernacular Humanism associated with Pitcairn and the older Ruddiman. He addresses the Muse as "dame" with cheerful familiarity, using a language that is more consistently Scots than most other parts of the poem. This mischievously familiar attitude to the Muse is not vulgarity, but controlled high spirits. It sets the tone for the ensuing description:

Sing then, how on the *fourth* of June,
Our *bells* screed aff a loyal tune,   played
Our antient castle shoots at noon
                    Wi' flag-staff buskit,
Frae which the soldier blades come down
                    To cock their musket.

(Note that "down", in spite of the spelling, is clearly to be pronounced in the Scots way, "doon".)

So off he goes, describing the noise, the pranks, the brulzies with the City Guard, with artful verve. The poet's self, introduced in the very first line, is present throughout, both as observer and as celebrant, and the introduction of his own comments adds to the spontaneity of the tone, as when he addresses the old cannon, Mons Meg:

Right seldom am I gi'en to bannin,   swearing
But, by my saul, ye was a cannon,
Cou'd hit a man, had he been stannin
                    In shire o' Fife,
Sax long Scots miles ayont *Clackmannan*,
                    And tak his life.

The note of personal wonder, rising to a climax on a line which opens with four monosyllabic words—"Sax long Scots miles ayont Clackmannan"—represents technique of a high order, from which Burns was to learn. At the end of the poem he returns to the Muse, reminding himself that the final stages of riotous celebration are not fit themes for her, who is accustomed to more conventional poetic aspects of the day's proceedings:

She'll rather to the fields resort,
Whare music gars the day seem short,   makes
Whare doggies play, and lambies sport
                    On gowany braes,   daisy-covered
Whare peerless Fancy hads her court,
                    And tunes her lays.

"Peerless Fancy" is deliberate, almost ironic, English poetic diction: the pastoral aspects of the celebration are more suitable for conventional poetic treatment than the more violent urban goings-on that he has been recounting. And on that note of mingled pastoral cheerfulness and ironic poetizing the poem concludes. (The diminutives "doggies" and "lambies", so characteristic of north-eastern Scottish speech, Fergusson probably picked up from his parents.)

Fergusson's next contribution to *The Weekly Magazine* was an epigram in English verse "On the Death of Dr Toshack of Perth, a great homourist", and two Shenstonian pastoral poems, "The Simile" and "Damon to his Friends". More interesting, though still not in Scots, was his "Burlesque Poem" entitled "The Canongate Playhouse in Ruins". This opens in the burlesque style we have already seen him use, but soon a rhetorical seriousness takes over and the poet's genuine regret for the loss of the playhouse and his nostalgic recollection of the plays that were performed there express themselves in a derivative but yet genuinely felt English poetic style:

> O Shakespeare! where are all thy tinsell'd kings,
> Thy fawning courtiers, and thy waggish clowns?
> Where all thy fairies, spirits, witches, fiends,
> That here have gambol'd in nocturnal sport,
> Round the lone oak, or sunk in fear away
> From the shrill summons of the cock at morn?
> Where now the temples, palaces, and towers?

The Shakespearean echoes here—from *Julius Caesar*, *Hamlet* and *The Tempest*—are not in the least burlesque. He remembers with emotion Tenducci's singing, and concludes the poem, more moved, we feel, than he set out to be, with a tribute.

> To the blest memory of happier times.

Sincerity of emotion does not in itself, however, make

great poetry, and at best this is interesting and competent verse.

Fergusson's "Caller (fresh) Oysters" appeared in *The Weekly Magazine* on 27 August 1772. It is another of his convivial poems. Its opening, a fine tribute to the Forth and its fishermen, shows him handling the "Standart Habby" stanza with a slowness and an openness not often found in this verse form:

> Of a' the waters that can hobble
> A fishin yole or salmon coble,   yawl; flat-bottomed
> And can reward the fishers trouble,   boat
>> Or south or north,
> There's nane sae spacious or sae noble
>> As Firth o' *Forth*.

He moves inland from the sea, from the Forth coast to Auld Reekie's oyster cellars, and soon we have one of his cosy Edinburgh interiors again:

> Whan big as burns the gutters rin,
> Gin ye hae catcht a droukit skin,   wet
> To *Lucky Middlemist*'s loup in,
>> And sit fu snug
> O'er oysters and a dram o' gin,
>> Or haddock lug.   ear

Lucky Middlemist or Middlemass kept a tavern in the Cowgate ("where the south pier of the bridge now stands", Chambers informs us in his *Traditions of Edinburgh*) which was a popular venue for "oyster parties" in Fergusson's day. The Forth was then renowned for its oysters, the largest and best being the "pandours", those caught near Prestonpans at the doors of the salt pans.

> At *Musselbrough*, and eke *Newhaven*,
> The fisher-wives will get *top livin*,
> Whan *lads* gang out on Sunday's even
>> To treat their *joes*,
> And tak of fat pandours a prieven,   large oysters; taste
>> Or *mussel brose*: . . .

The poem is more than an Edinburgh poem: it is a Forth poem. The language is a lively colloquial Scots, yet not too colloquial to refuse to admit classical references. He follows the stanza about Lucky Middlemists with this:

> When auld Saunt Giles, at aught
>   o'clock,
> Gars merchant lowns their chopies
>   lock,
> There we adjourn wi' hearty fock
>   To birle our bodles,
> And get wharewi' to crack our joke,
>   And clear our noddles.

causes to; fellows; shops — Gars merchant lowns their chopies lock,
people — There we adjourn wi' hearty fock
spend our coppers — To birle our bodles,

"Chopies" has the north-eastern diminuitive again; "birle our bodles" is vividly colloquial, as is "clear our noddles". Yet the very next stanza introduces the sun as Phoebus:

> When *Phoebus* did his windocks steek,
> How aften at that *ingle* cheek
> Did I my frosty fingers beek,
>   And taste gude fare?
> I trow there was nae hame to seek
>   Whan steghin there.

shut — When *Phoebus* did his windocks steek,
fireside — How aften at that *ingle* cheek
warm — Did I my frosty fingers beek,
gorging — Whan steghin there.

Phoebus is easily domiciled in a racy Scots. Fergusson deliberately uses the Scots "windocks" for "windows", "steek", "beek" and the expressive "steghin" with its emphatic guttural to end the stanza. It might be asked how he gets away with it, how he can associate Phoebus with windocks and ingle cheeks and the rest without sounding absurd. The answer lies surely in his simple confidence that it can be done. He is not showing off, he is not self-consciously and exhibitionistically drawing on a genteel classical tradition as Burns sometimes does. There is for him no reason why a vivid colloquial Scots should not be enriched by whatever classical dimension he feels inclined to add at any given moment. The run of the verse

is the guarantee of the naturalness and appropriateness of
that dimension. The flow is never stopped or altered, there
is no pause of wonder or special attention.

The poem ends with advice to those who cannot stand
very firmly after having twice emptied "the big ars'd
bicker" (a splendid vulgarity): mix oysters with your
drink and you'll carry it as well as any greedy priest or
vicar:

> A' ye wha canna stand sae sicker,   *so firmly*
> Whan twice you've took'd the
>   big ars'd bicker,   *emptied; drinking cup,*
> Mix *caller oysters* wi' your liquor,
>   And I'm your debtor,
> If greedy *priest* or drouthy *vicar*
>   Will thole it better.

The rhymes "sicker", "bicker", "liquor", "vicar" add an
air of merriment to the verse. Fergusson was highly skilled
in using rhyme for a variety of purposes, often comic. In an
earlier stanza he had summoned the reader to "prie"
("taste") an oyster as a cure for sickness in these words:

> Come prie, frail man! for gin thou   *taste; if*
>   *art sick*
> The oyster is a rare cathartic,
> As ever doctor patient gart lick
>   To cure his ails;
> Whether you hae the head or heart-ake
>   It ay prevails.

The comic rhymes give notice here that the poet's recom-
mendation of oysters as a sovereign remedy for all kinds of
illness is made in a fit of high spirits and is not to be taken
as solemn truth.

On 3 September 1772 *The Weekly Magazine* published a
poem by "J.S." (identified by Grosart as "probably John
Scott, a farmer") which showed the kind of impact
Fergusson's poems were having on the magazine's
readers:

> Is Allan risen fae the deid,
> Wha aft has tun'd the aiten reed,
> And by the muses was decreed
> To grace the thistle?
> Na; Fergusson's cam in his stead
> To blaw the whistle.

oaten

The poem continues for eleven more stanzas, recalling some of Fergusson's Scots poems, complimenting him on his "saft and sweet" verses, inviting him to visit him at Berwick if ever he should go there, and signing himself (though the poem is dated from Berwick) "Mid-Louthian Johnnie". The following week Fergusson's reply appeared, following the tradition of the verse-letter as developed by Hamilton of Gilbertfield and Ramsay. It is a skilful enough "occasional" piece, but his predecessors had done as well in this mode. More original in both style and content is "Braid Claith", which appeared in *The Weekly Magazine* on 15 October. It is a social satire, making the point that as far as public opinion is concerned clothes make the man:

> Ye wha are fain to hae your name
> Wrote in the bonny book of fame,
> Let merit nae pretension claim
> To laurel'd wreath,
> But hap ye weel, baith back and wame,
> In gude Braid Claith.

clothe yourself; stomach

The third stanza shows him using outrageous rhymes for ironic rather than purely comic purposes:

> Waesuck for him wha has na fek o't!
> For he's a gowk they're sure to
> geck at,
> A chiel that ne'er will be respekit
> While he draws breath,
> Till his four quarters are bedeckit
> Wi' gude Braid Claith.

alas; amount
fool;
scoff
fellow

The poem proceeds through a series of sharply etched scenes illustrating the poet's point, until it reaches its penultimate stanza and broadens out into generalizations:

> Braid Claith lends fock an
>   unco heese,   remarkable lift
> Makes mony kail-worms butter-flies,   caterpillars
> Gies mony a doctor his degrees
>   For little skaith;   effort
> In short, you may be what you please
>   Wi' gude Braid Claith.

The concluding stanza appears to derive from a passage in the Life of Richard Boyse in Colley Cibber's *Lives of the Poets*: "His extreme carelessness about his dress was a circumstance very inauspicious to a man who lives in that city [Edinburgh]. They are such lovers of this kind of decorum, that they will admit of no infringement upon it; and were a man with more wit than Pope, and more philosophy than Newton, to appear in their market-place negligent in his apparel, he would be avoided by his acquaintances, who would rather risk his displeasure than the censure of the public, which would not fail to stigmatize them, for associating with a man seemingly poor; for they measure poverty and riches, understanding, or its opposite, by exterior appearance."[3]

Here is how Fergusson turned this thought in ending his poem:

> For thof ye had as wide a snout on   though
> As *Shakespeare* or Sir *Isaac Newton*,
> Your judgment fouk wou'd hae a doubt on,
>   I'll tak my aith,
> Till they cou'd see ye wi' a suit on
>   O' gude Braid Claith.

"Snout" and "doubt" are clearly to be pronounced "snoot" and "doot". To introduce "Sir Isaac Newton" as a rhyme between "snout on" and "doubt on" and follow it

with "suit on" has of course the comic effect associated
with rhyming two monosyllabic words and one disyllabic
one and, as we have seen, it is the sort of thing Fergusson
liked to do. But the effect is not simply that of a comic
trick; the comedy adds to the irony to sum up the point of
the poem in mocking laughter.

Fergusson's next poem in *The Weekly Magazine*
appeared on 29 October 1772, "An Eclogue To the
Memory of Dr William Wilkie, late Professor of Natural
Philosophy in the University of St. Andrews". Wilkie,
whose kindness to Fergusson when he was a student has
already been discussed, died on 11 October, so the poet
lost no time in commemorating him. This time he did not
write in "Standart *Habby*" or adopt the comic elegy tradition of the "Epitaph on Habbie Simson" and "Bonny
Heck" to more serious purposes, nor did he write in neo-
classic English in imitation of Shenstone. The poem is
modelled on Ramsay's pastoral elegies, but it is an
altogether more assured performance than anything
Ramsay did in that style. Fergusson uses heroic couplets
with gravity and flexibility (though the lines are as a rule
end-stopped) and the Scots appears completely at home
in this verse form. This is something new in eighteenth-
century Scots poetry:

summer's gone . . .	Tho' simmer's gane, an' we nae langer view
clover	The blades o' claver wat wi' pearls o' dew.
	Cauld winter's bleakest blasts we'll
easily recover from	eithly cowr,
fuel; harvest	Our eldin's driven, an' our har'st is owr;
	Our *rucks* fu' thick are stackit i' the yard,
salted cow	For the *Yule-feast* a sautit mart's prepar'd;

The ingle-nook supplies the simmer fields,   fireside
An' aft as mony gleefu' maments yields.
Swyth man! fling a' your sleepy springs awa',   quick!
An' on your canty whistle gie's a blaw: merry; give us
Blythness, I trow, maun lighten ilka eie,   every eye
An' ilka canty callant sing like me.   every cheerful lad

This is Davie, replying to Geordie's announcement of his as yet unexplained sorrow. Scots names now replace classical names. Geordie answers Davie, explaining why he cannot sing cheerfully:

Na, na; a canty spring wad now impart
Just threefald sorrow to my heavy heart.
Thof to the *weet* my ripen'd aits had fawn,   though; wet; oats
Or shake-winds owr my rigs wi' pith had blawn,   strong winds
To this I cou'd hae said, "I carena by,"   I don't care
Nor fund occasion now my cheeks to dry.
Crosses like thae, or lake of warld's gear,   goods
Are naething when we tyne a friend that's dear. . . ..   lose

Fergusson is exercising his Scots in a new way, continuing his search for appropriate ways of using and extending it. This particular route proved a blind alley. The pastoral convention had really had its day by this time, and to lament Wilkie by having two shepherds mourn the death of a poetic and astronomically minded fellow shepherd is hardly the most effective way of writing a Scots elegy. Geordie explains to Davie:

> 'Twas na for weel tim'd verse or
>   sangs alane,
> *[every]* He bore the bell frae ilka shepherd
>   swain.
> *Nature* to him had gi'en a kindly lore,
> *[wonders]* Deep a' her mystic *ferlies* to explore:
> For a' her secret workings he could gie
> Reasons which wi' her principles agree.. . .

And Davie replies:

> *[such]* They tell me, Geordie, he had sic
>   a gift
> *[glanced;]* That scarce a starnie blinkit frae
> *[sky]*   the lift,
> But he wou'd some auld warld name
>   for't find,
> *[caused him to]* As gart him keep it freshly in his
>   mind: . . .

The conclusion tries to lift the poem to classical heights with a formal (and conventional) reference to Virgil:

> Scholars and bards *unheard of yet* shall come,
> And stamp memorials on his grassy tomb,
> Which in yon antient kirk-yard shall remain,
> Fam'd as the urn that hads the MANTUAN *swain*.

The speaker is hardly a shepherd now, and in spite of the reference to "yon antient kirk-yard" and the Scots "hads" for "holds" the tone has moved away from any sort of Scottish rural expression to something more conventionally "poetic" in the eighteenth-century English manner. The poem is interesting for what it tries to do. Parts of it are remarkably successful, as in such lines as

> Whase sangs will ay in Scotland be
>   rever'd,
> While *slow-gawn owsen* turn the   slow-moving oxen
>   flowr'ry swaird;
> While bonny *lambies* lick the dews of
>   spring,
> While *gaudsmen* whistle, or while   ploughmen
> *birdies* sing.

The lambies and birdies take their place quite naturally in a landscape which, though Scottish, owes something to Gray and Shenstone. But this note is not consistent in the poem, and as a whole it does not quite come off.

On 17 November 1772 *The Weekly Magazine* published Fergusson's "Hallow Fair". This was a conscious attempt by Fergusson to revive an older Scottish tradition of poetry of popular celebration as represented by "Peblis to the Play" and "Christ's Kirk on the Green". The latter is the first poem in the first volume of Watson's *Choice Collection*: it is in a nine-line stanza, alternating iambic octosyllables and iambic trisyllables, with the last line consisting of four emphatic beats, always ending with the words "that day". Here is its opening stanza as Watson printed it:

> Was ne'er in Scotland heard nor seen
>   such Dancing and Deray;   boisterous mirth
> Neither at *Faulkland* on the Green,
>   nor *Peebles* at the Play,
> As was of Wooers as I ween
>   at *Christ's Kirk* on a day:
> For there came *Katie* washen clean
>   with her new Gown of Gray,
>   *Full gay that day.*

Fergusson's "Hallow Fair" celebrates a market that has held about the time of Hallowmas (All Saints' Day, 1 November), generally in the first week of November but in 1772 beginning on 9 November, in the outskirts of Edinburgh. It opens:

At *Hallowmas*, whan nights grow lang,
    And *starnies* shine fu' clear, — stars
What fock, the nippin cauld to bang, — people; cold; overcome
    Their winter *hap-warms* wear, — wraps
Near Edinbrough a fair there hads, — is held
    I wat there's nane whase name is, — know
For strappin dames and sturdy lads,
    And cap and stoup, mair famous — bowl and flagon
            Than it that day.

The poem follows the tradition in its lively descriptions of individual encounters:

Here country John in bonnet blue,
    An' eke his Sunda's claise on,
Rins after Meg wi' *rokelay* new, — cloak
    An' sappy kisses lays on; — moist
She'll tauntin say, Ye silly coof! — fool
    Be o' your gab mair spairin; — mouth
He'll tak the hint, and criesh her loof — grease her palm
    Wi' what will buy her fairin,
            To chow that day. — eat

He continues with a phrase that Burns was to pick up in the opening line of "Tam o' Shanter":

Here chapmen billies tak their stand, — merchant fellows
    An' shaw their *bonny wallies*; — finery
Wow, but they lie fu' gleg aff hand — cleverly
    To trick the silly fallows;
Heh, Sirs! what cairds and tinklers come, — vagrants; tinkers
    An' *ne'er-do-weel* horse-coupers,
An' spae-wives fenzying to be dumb, — pretending
    Wi' a' siclike landloupers, — suchlike vagabonds
            To thrive that day.

He introduces an Aberdonian, speaking in an accent he must have known well from his parents and from his visits

to Aberdeenshire, with its characteristic "f" for "wh" and
its "ee" vowels:

> Here Sawny cries, frae Aberdeen;
>   "Come ye to me fa need: who
> "The brawest *shanks* that e'er were   stockings
>   seen
>   "I'll sell ye cheap and guid.   good
> "I wit they are as protty hose   know; pretty
>   "As come frae *weyr* or *leem*:   knitting needles or loom
> "Here tak a rug, and shaw's your
>   pose: savings
>   "Forseeth, my ain's but teem   empty
>   "An' light this day."

"Take a good bargain and show us your store of money:
forsooth, my own is but empty and light this day."
"Guid", incidentally, is to be pronounced (as it still is in
Aberdeenshire) "gweed".

After eight stanzas of lively description in a racy Scots,
Fergusson unexpectedly introduces—without abandoning his Scots diction—classical references:

> Whan *Phoebus* ligs in *Thetis* lap,   lies
>   Auld Reikie gies them shelter,
> Whare cadgily they kiss the cap,   gaily; drink
>   An' ca't round helter-skelter.
> *Jock Bell* gaed furth to play his
>   freaks,
>   Great cause he had to rue it,
> For frae a stark Lochaber aix
>   He gat a *clamihewit*,   severe blow
>   Fu' sair that night.

This playful and confident introduction of classical
deities into a Scots poem is something that Fergusson
could do and neither Ramsay nor Burns could. Burns
could be funny about Latona and Thetis, but not in the
middle of a Scots poem, only in a deliberately obscene
parody of formal neo-classic language, as in his "Ode to

Spring" set to a traditional Scots air but using for the most part a far from traditional Scots language:

> When maukin bucks, at early f——s,
>> In drewy glens are seen, Sir;
> And birds, on boughs, take off their m—s,
>> Amang the leaves sae green, Sir;
> Laton's sun looks liquorish on
>> Dame Nature's grand impetus,
> Till his p—go rise, then westward flies
>> To r–ger Madame Thetis.

Fergusson's classicism was more inward and more spontaneous, and though, as we have seen, he enjoyed burlesque and mock-heroic, his relation to the older Scottish vernacular humanist tradition enabled him to accommodate Phoebus and Thetis in Scots verse without making a self-conscious bawdy joke of it.

The "clamihewit", which Fergusson glossed as "severe blow", received by Jock Bell from a Lochaber axe, must have been delivered by a member of the City Guard, who carried these weapons. His first readers would have recognized the incident as a further illustration of Fergusson's by now well known personal war against that body of elderly Highland policemen. In a later stanza he describes the victim lying in the street after the assault, while members of the City Guard, speaking in a parody of a Highland accent, decide to take him into custody:

panting; street	He peching on the cawsey lay,
served	O' kicks and cuffs weel sair'd;
oath; gave	A *Highland* aith the serjeant gae,
must	"She maun pee see our guard."
warlike	Out spak the weirlike corporal,
	"Pring in ta drunken sot."
	They trail'd him ben, an' by my saul,
	He paid his drunken groat
next	For that neist day.

"To the Tron-kirk Bell" appeared in *The Weekly Magazine* in 26 November 1772. This is a poem in the old Scottish flyting tradition, a splendid piece of studied abuse directed at the "wanwordy [worthless], crazy, dinsome thing" whose "noisy tongue" was "sair to thole [endure]". Here Fergusson demonstrates a virtuosity that had not been seen in Scots poetry since the makars. The mixture of skill and gusto with which the bell is abused is reminiscent of Dunbar in his best flyting style. The poem, however, is not a satire on bells but on bailies: the conclusion is that the city fathers allow this scandal because they live out of its hearing:

If magistrates wi' me wad 'gree,	
For ay *tongue-tackit* shud you be,	tongue-tied
Nor fleg wi' *antimelody*	frighten
Sic honest fock,	folk
Whase lugs were never made to dree	ears; suffer
Thy doolfu' shock.	

But far frae thee the *bailies* dwell,	
Or they wud scunner at your knell,	feel disgust
Gie the *foul thief* his riven bell,	
And then, I trow,	
The by-word hads, "the de'il himsel'	holds
"Has got his due."	

An earlier stanza had described the bell as a trick of the Devil to scare people from church, and the concluding stanza comes round to the Devil again in a neat turn. Fergusson's ability to move a poem from its ostensible subject to a logical yet surprising conclusion becomes increasingly apparent in his Scots poems.

By the time "To the Tron-kirk Bell" appeared, Fergusson had already assembled a group of poems for publication in book form, so this poem was too late to be included in it. The publication date was probably January 1773; the title was simply *Poems by Robert Fergusson*. The

book contained twenty-seven poems in English and nine
in Scots ("Sandie and Willie", "Geordie and Davie",
"Elegy on the Death of Mr David Gregory", "The Daft-
Days", "The King's Birth-Day in Edinburgh", "Caller
Oysters", "Braid Claith", "Elegy on the Death of Scots
Music" and "Hallow-fair").

"Sandie and Willie, an Eclogue" had not appeared in
The Weekly Magazine. The poem is a dialogue between two
Scots farmers, Sandie complaining to Willie that his wife,
who seemed so modest and pretty and quiet when they
were courting, has turned out to be an idle scold. The
opening sets the scene in an assured Scots, domiciling the
English pastoral tradition firmly in Scotland:

	Twas e'ening whan the spreckled
goldfinch	gowdspink sang,
	Whan new fa'an dew in blobs o'
	chrystal sang;
	Than *Will* and *Sandie* thought they'd
	wrought enough,
oxen;	And loos'd their sair toil'd owsen
plough	frae the pleugh:
drove	Before they ca'd their cattle to the
	town,
	The lads to draw thir breath e'en sat
	them down:
oak	To the stiff sturdy aik they lean'd
	their backs,
	While honest Sandy thus began the cracks.

At a later point in the poem Sandie complains about his
wife's tea-drinking habits:

	Last ouk but ane I was frae hame
week	a day,
24 sheaves;	Buying a threave or twa o' bedding
straw	strae:
every	O'ilka thing the woman had her will,

Had fouth o' meal to bake, and hens   plenty
   to kill:
But hyn awa' to Edinbrough scoured she ran
To get a making o' her fav'rite tea;
And 'cause I left her not the weary
   clink   cash
She sell't the very truncher frae   wooden platters;
   my bink.   shelf.

To which Willie replies:

Her tea! ah! wae betide sic costly
   gear,
Or them that ever wad the price o't
   spear.
Sin my auld gutcher first the warld   grandfather
   knew,
Fouk had na fund the Indies, whare   folk had not found
   it grew.
I mind mysell, it's nae sae lang   remember
   sin syne,
Whan Auntie Marion did her stamack   lose her appetite
   tyne,
That *Davs* our gardiner came frae
   Apple-bogg,
An' gae her tea to tak by way o' drog.   drug

The growth of tea-drinking in eighteenth-century Scotland was viewed with suspicion by the conservative, and Fergusson seems to have shared this attitude. But what is of interest in this passage is less the reference to tea-drinking than the fluent colloquial tone shaped but not constricted by the supple iambic pentameters of the verse. The tone throughout is quietly objective; the speakers present themselves in a dramatic dialogue without the author's comment; they are not patronised or laughed at, yet the dialogue generates an air of realistic domestic comedy.

Willie listens sympathetically to Sandie's complaints, but refuses to interfere between man and wife:

> But mak or meddle betwixt man and wife,
> Is what I never did in a' my life.

He invites the unhappy Sandie to take his supper with him instead of at home:

drive;
oxen

these; bad-tempered

taste
husks of oats
boiled in water

> But yonder's Jock, he'll ca' your
>   owsen hame,
> And tak thir tidings to your thrawart
>   dame,
> That ye're awa' ae peacefu' meal to
>   prie,
> And take your supper kail or sowens
>   wi' me.

This poem is one of several that remind us that Fergusson, though a city poet, also knew and loved the country and was in touch with the rhythms of country life. He had seen farm life in Fife and Aberdeenshire, but, more important, he saw it all the time in the countryside around Edinburgh, for Edinburgh was still a small city with quick and easy access to its pastoral surroundings, as the ending of "The King's Birth-Day in Edinburgh" makes clear. It was not only the physical countryside that he was in touch with; it was also the spirit of rustic festivities and seasonal celebrations. In some respects these celebrations were common to town and country, and Fergusson can present them in either context. In his later poems "The Rising of the Session" and "The Sitting of the Session" he evokes vividly the effect on city life of the cessation and renewal of legal activity in that very legal city, and in "The Daft-Days" he describes the seasonal winter festivities of Edinburgh. But his more elemental feelings about seasonal change were both traditionally oriented and associated with the countryside.

Among the English poems in the 1773 volume that had

not appeared in *The Weekly Magazine* was the ambitious
Ode entitled "The Rivers of Scotland", which was set to
music by John Collett. This is in the tradition of the
eighteenth-century English ode, with different sections in
different rhythms. Incidental songs are punctuated by
choruses, some of the latter being set to traditional Scots
airs ("Tweedside" and "Gilderoy"). It is all rather forced
and over rhetorical. "Fortha's shores" harbour
"Naiades", "Pan from Arcadia to Tweda came", while

> From the dark wombs of earth Tay's waters spring,
>   Ordain'd by Jove's unalterable voice;
> The sounding lyre celestial muses string,
>   The choiring songsters in the groves rejoice.

There are patriotic outbursts, addresses to "Ye powers"
to protect "Scotia's ample fields" (Burns was to
remember "Ye Powers") and to Jove to keep foreign foes
from Caledon. The Ode seems to have been popular; it
was reprinted in three Edinburgh publications, *The
Nightingale* (1776), *The Goldfinch* (1777) and *The Scots
Nightingale* (1778), appealing as it did to a patriotic-
topographical-rhetorical taste, but it is pretty empty stuff
really.

Another English poem in the 1773 volume that had not
previously appeared is "The Town and Country Contrasted. In an Epistle to a Friend". Fifty-five lines of blank
verse contrasting in highly formal neo-classic English the
health-giving countryside with the smelly city end with a
moral appeal for "temperance, health's blyth con-
comitant". It is all very derivative, and "literary" in the
more dubious sense of the word.

The English poems in the 1773 volume also include an
"Ode to Hope" and an "Ode to Pity", the former
alternating heroic couplets with quatrains and the latter
entirely in octosyllabic couplets: there are echoes of both
Gray and Milton. There is also "A Tale", an amusing

anecdote in octosyllabic couplets where the major influence seems to be Matthew Prior. And there are a number of poems in anapaestic or dactylic quatrains with the lilting movement found in so many early eighteenth-century lyrics. These and other English poems in the volume show Fergusson aping a variety of styles, sometimes ingeniously, sometimes with a fair degree of craftsmanship, but never with the authority of his Scots poems.

That Walter and Thomas Ruddiman should have been prepared to issue a volume of young Fergusson's poems shows the esteem in which they held him by the end of 1772 and argues some degree of popularity for Fergusson's *Weekly Magazine* contributions. We know from other sources that his Scots contributions were widely esteemed, but there is no such evidence for the popularity of his English verses. Grosart says that he learned from a manuscript sketch of Fergusson's life by "Mr. Ruddiman" that the volume "was published by a subscription obtained in 1772, and that he sold upwards of five hundred copies, many of them at an advanced price". He adds that the poet "had a balance remaining of at least £50", which was a reasonable reward at the time. But the book cannot have been the success its publishers hoped. Grosart prints a letter from Fergusson's brother Hary, then serving on a ship on the American coast, which says: "When I arrive in England, I shall give you the necessary directions how to send your works, and make no doubt of selling them to advantage, when the ship is paid off."[4] This suggests that there were plenty of unsold copies. As there were no reviews of the book, we cannot be certain of its reception by the critics. We do not know the list of subscribers either, but we do know that Fergusson presented copies to James Boswell (with the inscription: "To James Boswell, Esq., the Friend of Liberty and Patron of Science; the following efforts of a Scottish youth are respectfully presented by his obedient and very humble servt. R. Fergusson"), the Earl of Glencairn (Burns's future patron), Sir Adam Fergusson of Kilkerran and David Herd, among others.

The volume was on the point of publication when Fergusson's poem "Good Eating" appeared in *The Weekly Magazine* on 17 December 1772. It is in the now familiar burlesque, mock-heroic style, which continued to have a fatal fascination for him. It opens:

> Hear, O ye host of Epicurus! hear!
> Each portly form, whose overhanging paunch
> Can well denote the all-transcendent joy
> That springs unbounded from fruition full
> Of rich repast; to you I consecrate
> The song advent'rous; . . .

He hails roast beef as "monarch of the festive throng", especially when accompanied

> By *root Hibernian*, or *plumb-pudding* rare,

and ends by recommending the reader to work up an appetite by walking by Arthur's Seat to Duddingston (then famous for its sheep-head dinners and today still boasting the Sheep-Heid Inn) or to Lawson's tavern on the shore at Leith:

> Ye who for health, for exercise, for air,
> Oft saunter from *Edina*'s smoke-capt spires,
> And, by the grassy hill or dimpl'd brook
> An appetite revive, should oft-times stray
> O'er *Arthur's seat's* green pastures to the town,
> For *sheep-heads* and bone-bridges fam'd of yore,
> That in our country's annals stands yclept,
> Fair *Duddingstonia*, where you may be blest
> With simple fare and vegetative sweets,
> Freed from the clamours of the busy world.
>   Or, if for recreation you should stray
> To *Leithian* shore, and breathe the keener air
> Wafted from Neptune's empire of the main;
> If appetite invite, and cash prevail,

> Ply not your joints upon the homeward track,
> Till LAWSON, chiefest of the Scottish hosts!
> To nimble-footed waiters give command
> The cloth to lay.. . . .

At this point the poem, which begins in a large general manner, becomes very much an Edinburgh affair, and that must have been part of its appeal to its first readers. It is perhaps surprising that Fergusson should have continued to celebrate his city in this English burlesque style after he had found and so successfully employed a Scots style so much more vigorous and authentic.

1773 opened with the publication in *The Weekly Magazine* of "The Delights of Virtue", a moralising piece in English quatrains whose movement suggests Gray's "Elegy". But on 21 January he returned to Scots, with one of his finest poems, "Caller Water", a poem in praise of fresh water which, deftly handled and cunningly constructed, turned out to be a poem in praise of the Edinburgh lasses. Water kept "father Adie" healthy in Eden (Fergusson uses that familiar tone in talking of scriptural characters that Burns was to exploit so happily); it is prescribed by doctors who confuse their patients' noddles by giving it a pretentious Latin name; it provides healthful swimming; it cures the colic; it keeps the lasses trig and bonny. The opening has a fine humorous directness:

> Whan father *Adie* first pat spade in
> The bonny yeard of antient Eden,
> His amry had nae liquor laid in
>   To fire his mou',
> Nor did he thole his wife's upbraidin'
>   For being fou.

cupboard

suffer
drunk

(The second line is echoed in the fifteenth stanza of Burns's "Address to the Deil"—"Lang syne in Eden's bonie yard"—both poets deliberately domiciling the remote biblical Garden of Eden in a familiar local context.)

Fergusson uses "feminine" rhymes in his characteristic way:

> Tho' cholic or the heart-scald   heartburn
>   teaze us,
> Or ony inward pain should seize us,
> It masters a' sic fell diseases
>   That would ye spulzie,   ravage
> And brings them to a canny crisis
>   Wi' little tulzie.   trouble

In the tenth stanza of this fifteen-stanza poem he turns to the beneficial effect of fresh water on "the bonny lasses" and he stays with this aspect until the end, concluding with a deft little turn to the poet himself, who modestly ends the final line:

> O may they still pursue the way
> To look sae feat, sae clean, sae gay!   pretty
> Than shall their beauties glance
>   like *May*,
>   And, like her, be
> The goddess of the vocal Spray,
>   The Muse, and me.

The language has become almost standard English now, and a phrase such as "goddess of the vocal Spray" taken out of context might sound like a high formal neo-classic English. Yet Fergusson's Scots can accommodate this kind of language; it is fluent and confident enough to allow him to include English in more ceremonial moments of the poem, as in this conclusion. A poem like "Caller Water" shows clearly how Fergusson found a way of developing a poetic vocabulary larger and more versatile than either a limited regional Scots or a standard neo-classic English, and this indeed is always an advantage open to a Scots poet. Fergusson did not invent this ability to move freely within both languages: the Middle Scots poets, too, could draw on an English vocabulary to enrich their Scots at appropriate moments. Burns was to do this too.

Fergusson's next Scots poem to appear in *The Weekly Magazine* was "Mutual Complaint of Plainstanes and Causey [pavement and street] in their Mother-tongue". It is a dialogue in octosyllabic couplets. (In content though not in verse-form this clearly influenced Burns's "The Brigs of Ayr"; the verse form is seen in Burns's "The Twa Dogs".) Each party in the dialogue complains of what it has to bear and thinks it has a worse lot than the other—causey with wagons, horses, coaches, Highland chairmen and the Luckenbooths, plainstanes (designed for nothing heavier than "sole of shoe or pump") trod by "burden-bearers heavy shoe" and loutish rustic characters. The result is both a picture of Edinburgh street life and a satire on snobbery. Each suggests taking his case before the Town Council, which gives Fergusson the opportunity to show off his knowledge of legal terminology:

> I dinna care a single jot
> Tho' summon'd by a shelly-coat,
> Sae leally I'll propone defences,
> As get ye flung for my expences;
> Your libel I'll impugn *verbatim*
> And hae a *magnum damnum datum*; . . .

sheriff's officer — Tho' summon'd by a shelly-coat,
vigorously; put forward — Sae leally I'll propone defences,
baffled — As get ye flung for my expences;

They finally agree to take the matter to the Robin Hood debating society, and the poem ends with Plainstanes agreeing to the suggestion just before dawn brings the first pedestrians and puts an end to the night-time conversation:

way

> Content am I—But east the gate is
> The sun, wha taks his leave of Thetis,
> And comes to wauken honest fock,
> That gang to wark at sax o'clock;
> It sets us to be dumb a while,
> And let our words gie place to toil.

The appearance of Thetis, emphasized in the half-comic rhyme, is yet another example of ease in introducing such classical references in a wholly familiar manner in a Scots context.

"The Rising of the Session", which appeared in *The Weekly Magazine* on 18 March, should be considered together with "The Sitting of the Session", which did not appear until 4 November. Fergusson's work as a legal copyist made him well aware that Edinburgh life revolved around the activities of the Law Courts, which sat for two terms in the year from 12 November to 12 March and from 12 June to 12 August, with a three weeks' break at Christmas and New Year. These two poems give a vivid account of the bustle and business brought about by the opening of the Court and of the emptying of the city (especially of its taverns) after the session closed. No more gin drinking at Rob Gibb's tavern, conveniently situated beside Parliament House:

> Nae body takes a morning dribb   drop of liquor
> O' *Holland gin* frae *Robin Gibb*;
> And tho' a dram to Rob's mair sib   glass of whisky; closely
>   Than is his wife,   related
> He maun take time to daut his *Rib*   must; pet
>   Till siller's rife.

No more coffee or wine-and-biscuit consuming at "Indian Peter's" establishment, also conveniently near Parliament House:

> This *vacance* is a heavy doom   vacation
> On *Indian Peter's* coffee-room,
> For a' his china pigs are toom;   pitchers; empty
>   Nor do we see
> In wine the sucker biskets soom   sugar; swim
>   As light's a flee.

Indian Peter was Peter Williamson, originally an Aberdonian who had been kidnapped as a child while playing on the quay there and was taken to America, where he had many adventures, which included being captured and scalped by Indians. He eventually managed to return to Scotland and settled in Edinburgh, where he opened a tavern before turning to bookselling, printing and publishing. He published the first Edinburgh Directory and established the first penny-post in the city.

"The Sitting of the Session" presents the other side of the picture, showing in brilliant detail the revived life of the city, with tavern-keepers and litigants in full cry. The poem begins with one of Fergusson's fine seasonal portraits of Edinburgh in November:

shorn	Phoebus, sair cow'd wi' simmer's hight,
cowers; earth	Cours near the YIRD wi' blinking light;
cold show the river banks	Cauld show the haughs nae mair bedight
clothes	Wi' simmer's claes,
brace; gloomy	They heeze the heart o' dowy wight That thro' them gaes.

This description of a November day in Edinburgh opens with "Phoebus", but brings the classical sun-god to earth, as it were, at once with the next words, "sair cow'd wi' simmer's hight", expressive economical Scots, five words that required eleven for Matthew McDiarmid to render into English "grievously shorn of his strength in climbing to his summer's meridian". The Scots continues in exuberant colloquial tone:

well know	The COURT O' SESSION, weel wat I,
puts every man's knife	Pitts ilk chiel's *whittle* i' the pye,
grease; slow-going	Can criesh the slaw-gaun wheels whan dry,
	Till Session's done,
	Tho' they'll gi'e mony a cheep and cry
twelfth	Or twalt o' June.

Ye benders a', that dwall in joot,   *drinkers; subsist on liquor*
You'll tak your liquor clean cap out,   *drunk off*
Synd your mouse-wabbs wi' reaming   *rinse; phlegm in throat;*
    stout,   *foaming*
        While ye ha'e cash,
And gar your cares a' tak the rout,   *make*
        An thumb ne'er fash.   *never trouble yourself*

ROB GIBB'S grey gizz, new frizzl'd   *wig; curled*
    fine,
Will white as ony snaw-ba' shine;
Weel does he lo'e the LAWEN coin   *money for payment of*
        Whan dossied down,   *tavern bill   paid*
For whisky gills or dribbs of wine   *drops*
        In cauld forenoon.

Drink and the law intermingle effortlessly:

Now at the door they'll raise a plea;
Crack on, my lads—for flyting's   *wrangling*
    free;
For gin ye shou'd tongue-tacket be,   *tongue-tied*
        The mair's the pity,
Whan scalding but and ben we see   *scolding backwards and*
        PENDENTE LITE.   *forwards*

The legal tag *pendente lite* (pending the result of the action) rhymes ironically with "mair's the pity". Is the poem about drink or about the law? Both can be dangerous, and the concluding stanza points the moral:

But LAW's a DRAW-WELL unco deep,
Withouten RIM fock out to keep: *people*
A donnart chiel, whan drunk, may   *stupid;*
    dreep   *fall*
        Fu' sleely in,   *easily*
But finds the gate baith *stay* and   *way; hard to climb*
    steep
        'Ere out he win.

Fergusson's next poem in *The Weekly Magazine* appeared on 8 April. It is in his familiar burlesque style, mock-heroic couplets, but the interest lies less in its somewhat undergraduate humour than in its subject: he is taking off Henry Mackenzie, the celebrated and popular author of the sentimental novel *The Man of Feeling*, a book that was to be passionately admired by Burns on whom it did not have a good influence. But Fergusson was more confident in his attitude to contemporary literary fashion than Burns was able to be, and he could laugh equally at Henry Mackenzie and Dr. Johnson, representatives of two very different strains in the literary culture of his day. A few weeks before the appearance of Fergusson's poem, Mackenzie's tragedy *The Prince of Tunis* was performed in Edinburgh to great applause, though there was some criticism of its excessive feeling. Fergusson gleefully mocks the whole cult of feeling associated with Mackenzie, putting the monologue into the mouth of a sensitive sow mourning the destruction by butchers of her husband and children:

> Thrice happy, had I liv'd in Jewish time
> When swallowing pork or pig was doom'd a crime;
> My husband long had blest my longing arms
> Long, long had known love's sympathetic charms!

"Love's sympathetic charms", a phrase that Burns would have swallowed whole, is rendered ludicrous when put into the mouth of a pig, as indeed is the whole concept of a "man of feeling" when applied to an animal that resigns life in sorrow, "to be number'd 'mongst the *feeling swine*". "The Sow of Feeling" is not a poem of any distinction, any more than Fergusson's poem "To Dr Samuel Johnson: Food for a new Edition of his Dictionary". But both are significant declarations of independence.

On 22 April 1773 *The Weekly Magazine* published Fergusson's "Epilogue, *spoken by* Mr Wilson, *at the Theatre-royal, in the Character of an* Edinburgh Buck". It is another of

Fergusson's efforts in mock-heroic couplets, and very much an Edinburgh poem:

> Next we approach'd the bounds of *George's square*,
> Blest place! No watch, no constables come there.. . .

George Square was built in the 1760s by James Brown (who called it after his brother George), just north-east of the Meadows which lay on the site of the old Burgh Loch, drained earlier in the century. Fergusson, like many other Edinburgh citizens in his time and later, pronounced the Meadows "Meedies" or "Meadus", as the rhyme indicates:

> Here then, my Bucks! how drunken fate decreed us
> For a nocturnal visit to the *Meadows*, . . .

The precise Edinburgh placing of the poem and its evidence of Fergusson's continued interest in the theatre represent its only real interest.

"Ode to the Bee", in octosyllabic Scots couplets, appeared on 29 April. It is a moral poem, advising that "feckless creature, man" to learn from the "instructive bee". The language and tone combine a nervous Scots with a neo-classic formality. The poem concludes:

> Like thee, by fancy wing'd, the Muse
> Scuds ear' and heartsome o'er the   early
>   dews,
> Fu' vogie, and fu' blyth to crap   glad; crop
> The winsome flow'rs frae Nature's lap,
> Twining her living garlands there
> That lyart time can ne'er impair.   grey

Nothing that Fergusson had yet written prepared his readers for "The Farmer's Ingle", which appeared in *The Weekly Magazine* on 13 May, 1773. This poem has long been known as the inspiration of Burns's "The Cotter's Saturday Night", but it is a remarkable work in its own right and in some respects is a better poem than Burns's.

The Spenserian stanza in which it is written he got from James Thomson and Shenstone, but he uses it with his own kind of Scots *gravitas*. The line and a half from Virgil's fifth Eclogue, which he uses as epigraph, describing indulgence in the joys of Bacchus by the fireside in cold weather, is perhaps an unnecessary classical flourish, but it gives evidence of the poet's working in an assured literary tradition. It is strange that Burns, who really was a peasant while Fergusson was not, wrote "The Cotter's Saturday Night" to show off some model rustics to benevolent genteel observers whereas Fergusson describes, with knowledge and affection, what he sees. Here at last is a full-blooded Scots poem, written by the whole man, rich and musical and confident:

	Whan gloming grey out o'er the
looks	welkin keeks,
	Whan *Batie* ca's his owsen to
	the byre,
exhausted;	And *Thrasher John* sair dung, his
shuts	barn-door steeks,
winnowing grain	And lusty lasses at the dighting
	tire:
overcomes; thoroughly	What bangs fu' leal the e'enings
	coming cauld,
makes; snow-topped	And gars snaw-tapit winter freeze
	in vain;
gloomy	Gars dowie mortals look baith blythe
	and bauld,
frightened; poverty	Nor fley'd wi' a' the poortith o'
	the plain;
	Begin, my Muse, and chant in hamely
	strain.

The slow, sonorous movement of the opening line effectively transforms into Scots the kind of feeling we get at the opening of Gray's "Elegy", but the stanza moves at once into particularization of Scots names that make the

rural activities real and local, not part of the sentimental
reverie of the observer. The invocation to "my Muse" in
the last line of the stanza might be expected to be pretentious or in some way out of place, but it is carried by the
movement of the verse and the tone of the whole stanza
without strain.

The second stanza describes the gudeman coming
home with a deliberate dropping of Scots words where
they fall most effectively—

> *Sods*, *peats*, and *heath'ry trufs* the   turfs
>   chimley fill,
> And gar their thick'ning smeek salute   make; smoke;
>   the lift; . . .   sky

The third stanza shows the gudewife making everything
ready for her man's arrival, with a relish of rustic fare that
is effortlessly tied to a generalization about hard work
requiring good food and drink (there is an echo back to the
epigraph from Virgil, but the difference between the
Virgilian and the Scottish festivity is as important as any
similarity):

> Weel kens the *gudewife* that the
>   pleughs require   ploughs
> A heartsome *meltith*, and refreshing   meal;
>   synd   drink
> O' nappy liquor, o'er a bleezing fire: strong ale
>   Sair wark and poortith douna weel be   poverty
>   join'd.
> Wi' butter'd *bannocks* now the *girdle*
>   reeks,   smokes
>   I' the far nook the *bowie* briskly   small barrel;
>   reams;   rises like cream
> The readied *kail* stand by the chimley
>   cheeks,
>   And had the riggin het wi' welcome   keep the roof hot
>   steams,
>   Whilk than the daintiest kitchen   which; relish
>   nicer seems.

The inversion of the last line here seems a bit forced, but then this is a formal poem, using a carefully wrought structure, and the kind of formality, even artificially, represented by this inversion, even though we may suspect that the verb is put at the end of the line for the sake of the rhyme, is not wildly out of place.

The fourth stanza moves to an unforced moralizing on the superior healthfullness of hard work and simple fare to idleness and drugs (a theme developed in the second canto of Thomson's *Castle of Indolence*, but handled here in tones of proverbial rustic wisdom rather than of genteel moralising) and the fifth develops this into a tribute to the achievements of Scotsmen of old, brought up on simple fare. Then, in the sixth stanza, he turns again to the scene before him:

sociable talk	The couthy cracks begin when supper's o'er
drinking cup;	The cheering *bicker* gars them
freely talk	glibly gash
moments of sunshine	O' simmer's *showery blinks* and winters sour,
farm;	Whase floods did erst their mailins
damage	produce hash:
	'Bout *kirk* and *market* eke their tales gae on,
	How *Jock* woo'd *Jenny* here to be his bride,
	And there how *Marion*, for a bastard son,
	Upo' the *cutty-stool* was forc'd to ride,
parish minister	The waefu' scald o' our *Mess John* to bide.

The last line of this stanza, like the last line of many of the stanzas, including the first, does not employ the Spenserian Alexandrine but uses the shorter pentameter. He uses the Alexandrine in only four stanzas, including the

SCOTTISH WRITERS 85

final one, in order to round the stanza off with a special weight or in some other way to involve the reader in the movement of a longer line, as in the description of the children quaking with fear when they hear stories of ghosts and warlocks:

> The fient a chiep's amang the bairnies now;   *devil a (i.e., not any)*
> For a' their anger's wi' their hunger gane:
> Ay maun the childer, wi' a fastin mou',   *must*
> Grumble and greet, and make an   *cry*
> unco mane,   *great moan*
> In rangles round before the ingle's   *groups; fire's blaze*
> low:
> Frae *gudame*'s mouth auld warld tale they hear,
> O' *Warlocks* louping round the *Wirrikow*,   *wizards; ghost*
> O' gaists that win in glen and   *live*
> kirk-yard drear,
> Whilk touzles a' their tap and gars   *tousles; top; makes*
> them shak wi' fear.

And so the evening wears on. In the tenth stanza we have an attractive picture of the gudeman relaxing, stretched out on a wooden settle with his cat and collie dog, and in the eleventh he is shown discussing the next day's work with the lads. In the twelfth stanza they all retire to bed, and the final stanza sounds an eloquent note of benediction:

> Peace to the husbandman and a' his tribe,
> Whase care fells a' our wants frae   *supplies*
> year to year;
> Lang may his sock and couter turn the   *ploughshare; coulter;*
> gleyb,   *glebe*
> And bauks o' corn bend down wi'   *strips of land*
> laded ear.

May SCOTIA's simmers ay look gay and
green,

harvests   Her yellow har'sts frae scowry
blasts decreed;

May a' her tenants sit fu' snug and

prosperous   bien,

Frae the hard grip of ails and

poverty   poortith freed,

And a lang lasting train o' peaceful
hours succeed.

This beautifully modulated ending rounds the poem off on a note that is both formal and colloquial. Lines such as "Lang may his sock and couter turn the gleyb" and "Her yellow har'sts frae scowry blasts decreed" and a simple colloquial phrase like "snug and bien" can lead up, without any trace of a false note, to the concluding Alexandrine, that swells out in an organ-noted benediction,

And a lang lasting train o' peaceful hours succeed.

Except for "lang" and perhaps "o'" this line could take its place easily in an English poem. But it is a tribute to Fergusson's mastery of his medium that it takes its place with equal ease in a poem written in Scots. For though "The Farmer's Ingle" is a Scots poem, this does not mean that it derives entirely and solely from Scottish literary tradition. On the contrary, the stanza form, the tone and even the subject show English influence; the significant point is that these influences have been thoroughly assimilated, and are used in an assured Scots way. The strength of a national art does not lie in its refusal to borrow from other national arts, but in its ability to domesticate its borrowings properly in its own medium. This is what Fergusson does in "The Farmer's Ingle", and it is something that no Scottish poet of the eighteenth century had yet done.

"The Ghaists: A Kirk-yard Eclogue" appeared in *The Weekly Magazine* on 27 May 1773. It is a dialogue between the ghosts of George Heriot and George Watson (Edinburgh merchants who had left bequests to found educational "hospitals"—now schools—in the city), who deplore the effect in Scotland of the proposed "Mortmain Bill" introduced in Westminster. The bill (which, as a result of Scottish opposition, was eventually restricted in scope to apply to England only) was intended to enable charitable foundations in Britain to realize their assets and invest the proceeds in three per cent funds, which would be the future source of their income. This would have impoverished certain Scottish foundations, and Scottish national feeling was aroused. Fergusson's poem was a contribution to the debate, and at the same time a defence of the national integrity of Scotland. (One is reminded of Walter Scott's *Letters of Malachi Malagrowther* in a later generation.) The verse is the heroic couplet, handled with considerable weight and flexible enough to accommodate such extremes as an echo of Hamlet ("But look, the Morn, in russet mantle clad . . .")—

> For tho' the eastern lift betakens day,   *sky*
> Changing her rokelay black for mantle   *cloak*
> grey—

and the spitting irony of

> Starving for England's weel at *three per cent.*

Here is Herriot's (as Fergusson spells the name) second speech:

> Think na I vent my well-a-day in vain.   *lament*
> Kent ye the cause, ye sure wad join
> my mane.
> Black be the day that e'er to England's
> ground
> Scotland was eikit by the UNION's   *increased*
> bond;

crowd	For mony a menzie of destructive ills
	The country now maun brook frae
	mortmain bills,
	That void our test'ments, and can
	freely gie
such; scope	Sic will and scoup to the ordain'd
	trustee,
strip;	That he may tir our stateliest
roofs	riggins bare,
	Nor acres, houses, woods nor fishins
	spare,
staggering	Till he can lend the stoitering state
	a lift
gold in handfulls	Wi' gowd in gowpins as a grassum gift;
	In lieu o' whilk we maun be weel content
	To tyne the capital at three *per cent*.. . .
whole	Hale interest for my fund can
	scantly now
clothe; boys; stop	Cleed a' my callants backs, and stap
	their mou'.
must; stomachs;	How maun their weyms wi' sairest
sorest hunger	hunger slack,
shabby clothes;	Their duds in targets flaff upo'
tatters; flap	their back,
	Whan they are doom'd to keep a lasting
	Lent,
	Starving for England's weel at *three*
	per cent.

(A "grassum gift" is a fee paid by the landlord to the incoming tenant: under the proposed legislation the trustees would abandon the secure position of landlord for the less secure position of tenant.)

This kind of patriotic poetry, dealing with contemporary affairs, is both more poetic and more effective than the oblique pseudo-historical contrivances of Allan Ramsay.

For all his successes with Scots poetry by this time, Fergusson was still enamoured of the English burlesque, mock-heroic style, and he returned to it again with "The Bugs", which appeared in *The Weekly Magazine* on 10 June 1773. What was it that so fascinated him about this rather childish form of poetic humour? Was it that he was most at home in an English poetic style when it contained an element of parody? Was there a streak of the incorrigible undergraduate persisting in him? The traditions handed down about Fergusson's life in Edinburgh suggest that there is certainly some truth in the latter diagnosis; he was a great practical joker and he liked to abandon himself to the moment of convivial celebration. And he was still a very young man: he was only twenty-four when he died. But it may well be true that there was a more serious element in his constant recurring to English mock-heroic burlesque, that he wanted to keep the English poetic tradition at arm's length and that he could best do this by employing an English style in which he could simultaneously exhibit a certain virtuosity and mock the very style he was successfully employing. Of course it might be asked why English poets of the first half of the eighteenth century employed such a style—it was, after all, from them that Fergusson learned it. This is a complex question, and part of the answer seems to be that on the one hand neo-classic critical theory postulated the epic or heroic as the highest poetic mode while on the other hand the social tone of the age of Queen Anne, and the "Queen Anne Wits" who dominated London literary culture in the early years of the century, and who were really responsible for the emergence of the English eighteenth-century mock-heroic style, were a group of urban sophisticates who theoretically worshipped Homer as the great father of poetry while living in a world as far removed from the Homeric age as could be imagined. Fergusson's Edinburgh was different; but Fergusson had his own cultural reasons for employing a mode developed earlier in the

century by English poets to cope with the difference
between their poetic theory and their cultural situation. It
was not, however, the mode in which he realised his true
poetic potential.

On 11 June 1773 *The Perthshire Magazine of Knowledge and
Pleasure* printed a verse letter addressed to Fergusson by
Andrew Gray (who may have been, but who cannot be
certainly identified with, the scholar, humourist and
minister Dr. Andrew Gray), written in the "Standart
Habby" stanza which had by now become the accepted
stanza for Scots verse letters. This undistinguished poem
praises Fergusson for choosing to write in a popular Scots
while he could have written in elegant English if he had
wanted to:

> Ye've English plain enough nae doubt,
> And Latin too, but ye do suit
> Your lines, to fock that's out about
>   'Mang hills and braes:
> This is the thing that gars me shout
>   Sae loud your praise.

people

makes

Fergusson replied in the same magazine on 2 July. It is a
friendly poem, written in the same stanza and in the same
manner as Gray's, inviting Gray to a convivial session
with him. There is no doubt that Fergusson did not have
the special mastery of the verse letter that Burns was to
show: Burns had the ability to combine the informal tone
of a friendly letter with the formal structure of a deftly
organized poem that moved from a picture of the author
writing to the world outside, to make, at the centre of the
poem, some ringing statement about life before returning
to the local scene and the poet about to sign off.
Fergusson's verse letters are pleasant enough, but he did
better in other Scots forms.

Fergusson's next poem in *The Weekly Magazine* was "On
Seeing a Butterfly in the Street", written in octosyllabic
Scots couplets. It is a skilful translation into Scots of an

early eighteenth century English poetic mode, describing a butterfly—"Daft gowk in MACARONI dress"—that has flown from the country into the city, "To cast a dash at REIKIE's cross", and there finds itself quite out of place. The moral is that people should mind their own business and not stray into inappropriate places. "Hame Content. A Satire", which appeared on 8 July, is also in octosyllabic Scots couplets, but though it is in its way a moral poem it is more complex than the butterfly poem. One of its main themes is his determination to celebrate his native country rather than write of classical scenes:

> The ARNO and the TIBUR lang
> Hae run fell clear in Roman sang;
> But, save the reverence of schools!
> They're baith but lifeless dowy pools,   gloomy
> Dought they compare wi' bonny Tweed,
> As clear as ony lammer-bead?   amber-bead
> Or are their shores mair sweet and gay
> Than Fortha's haughs or banks o' Tay?   low ground at riverside

The poem turns into a celebration of the Scottish scene as a theme for Scottish songs and concludes with a lament for William Hamilton of Bangour, who had died in 1754 and whose song "The Braes of Yarrow", referred to in Fergusson's poem, was to inspire Wordsworth. The poem is neo-classic in tone, for all its aggressively Scottish feeling (Fergusson, unlike Ramsay and Burns, did not find these two incompatible), and moves with a certain ease from a vigorous Scots to a formal English vocabulary, as in the conclusion:

> O BANGOUR! now the hills and dales
> Nae mair gi'e back thy tender tales!
> The birks on Yarrow now deplore   birch-trees
> Thy mournfu' muse has left the shore:
> Near what bright burn or chrystal spring
> Did you your winsome whistle hing?   hang

The muse shall there, wi' WAT'RY eie,
Gi'e the dunk swaird a tear for thee;
And Yarrow's genius, dowy dame!
Shall there forget her blude-stain'd
        stream,
On thy sad grave to seek repose,
Wha mourn'd her fate, condol'd her woes.

moist-sward
gloomy

This has the precise feel of Collin's "Ode Written in the Beginning of the Year 1746", that perfectly chiselled little poem of two six-line stanzas, which ends:

By fairy hands their knell is rung,
By forms unseen their dirge is sung;
There Honour comes, a pilgrim gray,
To bless the turf that wraps their clay,
And Freedom shall a while repair
To dwell a weeping hermit there!

In "Hame Content" this tone is achieved as a final turn to a poem that moves through a series of moods, some of them satirical rather than elegiac, and very colloquial in accent:

Unyoke then, man, an' binna sweer
To ding a hole in ill-haind gear;
O think that EILD, wi' wyly fitt,
Is wearing nearer bit by bit;
Gin yence he claws you wi' his paw,
What's siller for? Fiend haet awa,
But GOWDEN playfair, that may please
The second SHARGER till he dies.

don't be reluctant
drive; uselessly hoarded
old age; cunning foot

if once
money

The concluding two-and-a-half lines of this passage (saying that once a man is dead his money will only go to the "sharger", the weakling, who inherits his wealth, until he in turn dies—"dies" to be pronounced "dees", as the rhyme indicates), and the ironic question "What's siller for?" that precedes them, show Fergusson master of a lively, colloquial satirical mood, which he skilfully modulates as the poem proceeds to move through patriotic celebration of elegy. Fergusson is in control throughout the poem, and knows precisely what he wants to do, and does it effectively.

Fergusson's next poem to appear in *The Weekly Magazine*, on 22 July, was "Leith Races", in the old Scottish tradition of poetry of popular festivity and using the same old stanza form he had used in "Hallow-Fair". It is best known today as the model for Burn's "Holy Fair", but it is a fine celebratory poem in its own right.

The poem begins with an encounter. This is very much in the ballad tradition, as Matthew McDiarmid has noted, but it is also in a tradition that is much more widespread than the ballad, the old mediaeval tradition of the poet beginning by narrating his going forth into a wood or the fields and meeting with someone who provides the reason for the poem. Where Fergusson got this from we cannot precisely say; it may be that he thought it up for himself and thus unconsciously made contact with an age-old poetic mode. The poem begins with a meeting in a July country setting:

> In JULY month, ae bonny morn,   one
>   Whan Nature's rokelay green   cloak
> Was spread o'er ilka rigg o' corn   every ridge
> To charm our roving een;   eyes
> Glouring about I saw a quean,   girl
>   The fairest 'neath the lift;   sky
> Her EEN ware o' the siller sheen,
>   Her SKIN like snawy drift,
>   Sae white that day.
>
> Quod she, "I ferly unco sair,   marvel very much
>   "That ye sud musand gae,   should musing
> "Ye wha hae sung o' HALLOW-FAIR,
>   "Her winter's pranks and play:
> "Whan on LEITH-SANDS the racers rare,

> "Wi' Jocky louns are met,
>
> spare; spend   "Their orro pennies there to ware,
>
> "And drown themsel's in debt
>
>   "Fu' deep that day."

The use of the old Scots present participle in "musand" gives notice that this is to be a very Scottish—one might say a fiercely Scottish—poem. This is borne out in the ensuing stanzas. The poet asks the "quean" who she is:

> An' wha are ye, my winsome dear,
> That takes the gate sae early? . . .

The poet has a right to ask, for he is now known as a poet and has been greeted by the girl as the author of "Hallow-Fair". She replies that she is Mirth—not a generalized allegorical Mirth, but a very Scottish character:

fresh   "I dwall amang the caller springs

moisten   "That weet the LAND O' CAKES,

merry   "And aften tune my canty strings

> "At BRIDALS and LATE-WAKES:
> "They ca' me MIRTH; I ne'er was kend
> "To grumble or look sour,
> "But blyth wad be a lift to lend,

prove   "Gif ye wad sey my pow'r
>   "An' pith this day."

With this, Mirth has served her function in the poem. The poet agrees to be her companion in rambling through Leith and Edinburgh to see the popular merry-making associated with Leith races:

> We'll reel and ramble thro' the sands,
> And jeer wi' a' we meet;

miss   Nor hip the daft and gleesome bands
> That fill EDINA's street
>   Sae thrang this day.

We hear no more of the guide. The poet is now the observer and recorder of popular merriment. The ladies who rise early to put on their "brawest ribbons", the "scaw'd and bare-ars'd lowns" who also rise early and proceed to frighten the town "wi' dinsome squeel and bark", the announcement of the horses and riders:

> "Here is the true an' faithfu' list
>   "O' Noblemen and Horses;
> "Their eild, their weight, their   age;
>   height, their grist,   size
> "That rin for PLATES or PURSES
>   "Fu' fleet this day."

And of course there is the City Guard, its members newly shaved and their limbs "dight in spaterdashes" instead of in their usual "filibegs", speaking in that parodic Gaelic English that was associated with them:

> Her *Nanesel* maun be carefu' now,   must
>   Nor maun she pe misleard,   ill-bred
> Sin baxter lads hae seal'd a vow   baker
>   To skelp and clout the guard: . . .

And on we go, at a rapid pace, past "tinkler billie's in the Bow", "burrochs" reeling down Leith Walk, "browster wives" who

>   thegither harl   drag
>   A' trash that they can fa' on;
> They rake the grounds o' ilka barrel,
>   To profit by the lawen: money

"Buchan bodies" crying their "Findrums" (small dried haddocks) in their north-east dialect—

> "gueed speldings, fa will buy"—

"wylie wights" playing "Rowly Powl" and throwing dice, gilded whores in hackney carriages, until the end of the day when, tired and drunk,

> Great feck gae hirpling hame like   staggering
>   fools,
>   The cripple lead the blind.

The final stanza ends with a wish that drink might never
make folk bad-tempered enough to enter into quarrels and
end up with a black eye:

> May ne'er the canker o' the drink
> bad-tempered   E'er make our spirits thrawart,
> 'Case we git wharewitha' to wink
> eyes; blue-bell   Wi' een as BLUE's a BLAWART
> blows   Wi' *straiks* thir days!

The poem is essentially a series of brightly coloured
pictures, each one drawn vividly and jocularly and each
succeeding the other in rapid movement. The effect is like
the translation of a Breughel picture into a moving film.
There is a sense of openness to life, an amused tolerance of
follies and excesses, a satirical tone that is at the same time
friendly and participatory, that make this poem more
than an exercise in an old tradition of poetry of popular
merry-making. Burns was to recapture precisely this combination of qualities in his "Holy Fair". How far below
this Fergusson could fall when, instead of drawing on a
lively old Scots tradition, he drew on a somewhat debased
English tradition of poetry of conviviality, can be seen if
we set a poem such as "Leith Races" beside a song he
wrote (to the air, "Lumps of Pudding") about the same
time:

> HOLLO! keep it up, boys—and push round the
> glass,
> Let each seize his bumper, and drink to his lass:
> Away with dull thinking—'tis madness to think—
> And let those be sober who've nothing to drink.
> Tal de ral &c.

As Dr. Johnson said of Macpherson's Ossian, a man could
write such stuff for ever if he would abandon his mind to it.

Fergusson had not yet done with the English burlesque,
mock-heroic mode. He was at it again in *The Weekly
Magazine* of 5 August 1773 in a poem entitled "Tea". It
opens with one enormous sentence:

YE maidens modest! on whose sullen brows
Hath weaning chastity her wrinkles cull'd,
Who constant labour o'er consumptive oil
At midnight knell, to wash sleep's nightly balm
From closing eye-lids, with the grateful drops
Of TEA's blest juices; list th'obsequious lays
That come not with Parnassian honours crown'd
To dwell in murmurs o'er your sleepy sense,
But fresh from ORIENT blown to chace far off
Your LETHARGY, that dormant NEEDLES rous'd
May pierce the waving MANTUA's silken folds:
For many a dame, in chamber sadly pent,
Hath this reviving liquid call'd to life;
And well it did, to mitigate the frowns
Of anger reddening on *Lucinda*'s brow
With flash malignant, that had harbour'd there,
If she at masquerade, or play, or ball,
Appear'd not in her newest, best attire,
But VENUS, goddess of th'eternal smile,
Knowing that stormy brows but ill become
Fair patterns of her beauty, hath ordain'd
Celestial Tea.

The "Ode to the Gowdspink" followed on 12 August, in Scots octosyllabic couplets this time, in a style similar to that employed in "On Seeing a Butterfly in the Street". It is a simply moral poem: the caged goldfinch, though fed abundantly and maintained in comfort, pines without his freedom. The feel of the poem is English though the language is Scots. Then, on 26 August, he turns yet again to the burlesque mock-heroic style, in "An Expedition to Fife and the Island of May, on board the Blessed Endeavour of Dunbar, Captain Roxburgh Commander". It is in fact one of the most successful of Fergusson's poems in this dubious mode, ending with abuse of Fife and praise of Lothian:

To FIFE we steer, of all beneath the sun
The most unhallow'd 'midst the SCOTIAN plains!
And here, sad emblem of deceitful times!
Hath sad hypocrisy her standard borne.
Mirth knows no residence, but ghastly fear
Stands trembling and appall'd at airy sights.
ONCE, only *only once*! Reward it, O ye powers!
Did HOSPITALITY, with open face,
And winning smile, cheer the deserted sight,
That else had languish'd for the blest return
Of beauteous day, to dissipate the clouds
Of endless night, and superstition wild,
That constant hover o'er the dark abode.
O happy LOTHIAN! Happy thrice her sons!
Who ne'er yet ventur'd from the southern shore,
To tempt misfortune on the *Fifan* coast,
Again with thee we dwell, and taste thy joys,
Where sorrow reigns not, and where every gale
Is fraught with fullness, blest with living hope,
That fears no canker from the year's decay.

On 2 September 1773 Fergusson returned to Scots with
a poem in *The Weekly Magazine* entitled "To the Principal
and Professors of the University of St Andrews, on their
superb treat to Dr Samuel Johnson". This was a
characteristic piece of nose-thumbing at the Establishment. Dr Johnson, starting on his famous tour of the
Western Isles with Boswell, was first proceeding up the
east coast of Scotland. They visited St. Andrews where, as
Boswell duly noted, "the professors entertained us with a
very good dinner" on 19 August. Fergusson had an affection but no great veneration for his *alma mater*, while his
feelings about Johnson were affected by Johnson's known
anti-Scottish views. Here was an opportunity to write a
satiric poem in assertive Scots putting the great man and
his hosts in their place. The tone is deliberately disrespect-
ful: Dr. Johnson is "Sammy":

St Andrews town may look right gawsy,   *stately*
Nae GRASS will grow upon her cawsey,   *street*
Nor wa'flow'rs of a yellow dye,
Glour dowy h'er her RUINS high,   *gaze*
Sin SAMY's head weel pang'd wi' lear   *crammed; learning*
Has seen the ALMA MATER there:
Regents, my winsome billy boys!
'Bout him you've made an unco noise;
Nae doubt for him your bells wad clink,
To find him upon EDEN's brink,
An' a' things nicely set in order,
Wad keep him on the Fifan border:
I'se arrant now frae France an' Spain
Baith COOKS and SCULLIONS mony ane
Wad gar the pats an' kettles tingle   *make; pots*
Around the college kitchen ingle   *fire*
To fleg frae a' your craigs the roup,   *frighten; throats;*
Wi' reeking het and crieshy soup;   *hoarseness   greasy*
And *snails* and *puddocks* mony hunder   *frogs*
Wad beeking lie the hearth-stane under,   *warming*
Wi' roast and boild, an' a' kin kind,
To heat the body, cool the mind.

But if he had been there, the poet would have arranged a purely Scottish diet. He remembers that Johnson had defined oats in his Dictionary as a food given to horses in England and eaten by men and women in Scotland. Let him then learn something more about Scottish food. His proposed menu begins with

a haggis fat,
Weel tottl'd in a seything pat,   *boiled; boiling pot*
Wi' *spice* and *ingans* weel ca'd thro', . . .   *onions*

and continues with "a gude sheep's head", then some "gude fat brose", washing it down with "the contents o' sma' ale quegh".

grimace	Then let his wisdom girn an' snarl
oat cake	O'er a weel-tostit girdle farl,
in spite of his stomach	An' learn, that maugre o' his wame,
	Ill bairns are ay best heard at hame.

The poem proceeds to lament that Scotland "maun stap ilk birky's mow" with foreign "eistacks" (dainties) when her native peasantry made do with "cog o' brose an' cutty spoon". If, he concludes, critics accuse him of being unfair to Fife (not, significantly, of being unfair to Dr. Johnson), then let them come and drink with him, and the process will improve their prose "and heal my rhyme".

The poem races along with high satiric exuberance, the Scots words almost shouting their native vigour at the anti-Scottish doctor. It is a joke, a show of high spirits, a Scottish nationalist exhibition piece, an "occasional" poem. It is not the finest kind of poetry of which Fergusson was capable, but it is first-rate of its kind.

On 16 September *The Weekly Magazine* published Fergusson's poem on the Town Council elections, entitled simply "The Election". It is in the old Scottish stanza he had used in "Leith Races" and gives a humorously mocking account of the activities of election day. Burns was to remember some of Fergusson's vivid phrases:

hasten	The DEACONS at the counsel stent
	To get themsel's presentit:
two years; soul	For towmonths twa their saul is lent
	For the town's gude indentit: . . .

The last phrase is echoed in Burns's "The Twa Dogs":

perhaps; busy	Wha aiblins, thrang a-parliamentin'
	For Britain's gude his saul indentin . . .

Fergusson's next poem to appear in *The Weekly Magazine*, "Elegy on John Hogg, late Porter to the University of ST ANDREWS", is very much a St. Andrews poem, full of local allusions and university reminiscences.

It is in the "Standart *Habby*" form, and again it shows
Fergusson adapting a tradition of mock elegy to a more
serious mood, though here the tone of jovial reminiscence
overcomes the note of loss and the mood is almost that of a
wake, combining mourning and festivity. It is a deftly
poised poem, and shows how fluently Fergusson could
now handle this old Scottish verse form.

The Weekly Magazine of 21 October published
Fergusson's second poem laughing at Dr. Johnson, "To
Dr SAMUEL JOHNSON: Food for a new Edition of his
DICTIONARY". Here Fergusson's fondness for burles-
que finds vent in a somewhat schoolboyish parody of Dr.
Johnson's fondness of a Latinized vocabulary:

> GREAT PEDADOGUE, whose literanian lore,
> With SYLLABLE and SYLLABLE conjoin'd
> To transmutate and varyfy, has learn'd
> The whole revolving scientific names
> That in the alphabetic columns lie,
> Far from the knowledge of mortalic shapes,
> As we, who never can peroculate
> The miracles by thee miraculiz'd,
> The Muse silential long, with mouth apart
> Would give vibration to stagnatic tongue,
> And loud encomiate thy puissant name,
> Eulogiated from the green decline
> Of Thames's banks to Scoticanian shores,
> Where Loch-lomondian liquids undulize.

On 4 November *The Weekly Magazine* published an
"Extract of a letter from Inverary" telling how Johnson
and Boswell were storm-bound on the Isle of Coll for a fort-
night and quoting Johnson's praise of the benevolence of
the Highlanders which concluded, "I love the people
better than the country". Immediately following this news
item is an epigram on the subject by Fergusson, who must
have seen the item or heard about its contents before it was
printed for clearly his compliment to Johnson, so different

from the attitude he had displayed earlier, resulted from a softened attitude to the sage. That this was produced by a report suggesting that Johnson after all loved the Scots shows how important to Fergusson the national issue was and how much he tended to judge Englishmen by their attitude to the Scots. The epigram is in neo-classic English: he is paying Johnson the compliment of using his (Johnson's) language instead of assailing him with an onslaught of Scots as he had previously done:

> TWO GEMS, the nation's greatest boast,
>   To Scotia's plains drew near,
> Bright to illume her dismal coast,
>   And barren fields to cheer.
>
> She, fearing that their gracious forms,
>   To other climes would fly,
> LEARNING and LIBERTY by storms
>   Confin'd to ISLE of SKY.

(Of course it is quite possible that the poem is entirely ironical, which would make nonsense of the argument above.)

On 11 November *The Weekly Magazine* printed Fergusson's poem "A Drink Eclogue. Landlady, Brandy and Whisky". This is a flyting, in Scots heroic couplets, between Brandy and Whisky. Brandy sneers at Whisky as the drink of "porters, chairmen, city-guard" (all of whom tended to be Highlanders: chairmen were the men who carried sedan chairs) and boasts of its own superior breeding; Whisky complains that the gentlefolk nowadays despise their native spirit and prefer imported stuff:

home-bred   Yet I am hameil, there's the sour
                   mischance!
               I'm no frae Turkey, Italy, or France;
mouths   For now our Gentles gabbs are grown
                   sae nice,

> At thee they toot, an' never speer my   drink; ask
>> price:
> Witness—for thee they hight their
>> tenants rent,
> And fill their lands wi' poortith,   poverty
>> discontent;
> Gar them o'er seas for cheaper mailins   farms
>> hunt,
> An' leave their ain as bare's the
>> Cairn-o'mount.

There is social criticism here, as well as the same kind of complaint about the rejection of native traditions that we find in the "Elegy, On the Death of Scots Music". Brandy replies that the drinking of brandy by landlords is not the cause of tenants' poverty, which is caused by the tenants' love of whisky:

> For love to you, there's mony a tenant
>> gaes
> Bare-ars'd and barefoot o'er the
>> Highland braes:
> For you nae mair the thrifty gudewife
>> sees
> Her lasses kirn, or birze the dainty   churn; press
>> cheese;
> CRUMMIE nae mair for Jenny's hand
>> will crune   low
> Wi' milkness dreeping frae her teats
>> adown:
> For you o'er ear' the ox his fate
>> partakes,
> And fa's a victim to the bludey aix.

This passage contains an echo of Gray's "Elegy":

> For them no more the blazing hearth shall burn,
>> Or busy housewife ply her evening care;
> No children run to lisp their sire's return,
>> Or climb his knees the envied kiss to share.

Yet Fergusson's tone is not Gray's, and there is nothing in the mournful flow of Gray's lines to compare with Fergusson's harsh line

> And fa's a victim to the bludey aix.

Whisky retorts that it is Brandy that makes greedy bankers embezzle the maiden's dowry; Brandy abuses Whisky as a "haveril Scot"

> that for ay maun dwell
> In poet's garret, or in chairman's
>   cell,
> While I shall yet on bien-clad tables
>   stand,
> Bouden wi' a' the daintiths o' the
>   land.

well-furnished

laden

Whisky replies by boasting of the inspiration it has given to poets, notably Allan Ramsay ("Allie"), and then Brandy summons the landlady to decide the issue between them. The landlady points out that

deficiencies

> Inlakes o' BRANDY we can soon supply
> By WHISKY tinctur'd wi' the SAFFRON's
>   dye,

and turns on Brandy:

> Will you your breeding threep, ye
>   *mongrel loun*!
> Frae hame-bred liquor dy'd to colour
>   brown?
> So FLUNKY braw, whan drest in master's
>   claise,
> Struts to Auld Reikie's cross on sunny
>   days,
> Till some auld comerade, ablins out o'
>   place,
> Near the vain upstart shaws his meagre
>   face;

perhaps

Bombaz'd he loups frae sight, and jooks his ken,   *gets quickly out of the way*
Fley'd to be seen amang the tassel'd train.   *frightened*

This is an unexpected turn at the end. Not only is Brandy dismissed as an upstart, merely whisky died yellow or brown ("brown", by the way, is clearly to be pronounced "broon"), but the analogy is then made with upstart flunkies parading at the Cross of Edinburgh, and the poem ends on a note of social satire. We have already seen Fergusson's skill at moving a poem round from its ostensible subject to its true subject; here the movement is done with great speed and neatness.

Two poems by Fergusson appeared in *The Weekly Magazine* of 25 November 1773, "To my Auld Breeks", a ruefully comic address to his worn-out trousers in Scots octosyllabic couplets, and "Rob. Fergusson's Last Will", in English octosyllabic couplets. A "Codicile to Rob. Fergusson's Last Will", also in English octosyllables but interlarded with Latin legal phrases, appeared on 23 December. It was his last contribution, and the poem itself, like the previous one, though sounding a note of rather forced humour, is some indication of his foreboding of death. A letter to a friend written in October 1773 is subscribed "Your afflicted humble servant", while a verse letter addressed to Charles Lorimer refers to his gloomy state, says that he has given up drink in the fear that he would be attacked by "new horrors", but looks forward to the time when he will be restored to health and be sociable again.

It seems clear that Fergusson suffered a series of fits of depression from the autumn of 1773 and that he was also physically ill at least intermittently. He seems to have given up his duties at the Commissary Office after 30 December 1773. His absence from social gatherings in Edinburgh was remarked by his friends, and the cessation of his regular contributions to *The Weekly Magazine* was also noted with regret. Alexander Peterkin's biography of Fergusson, published in 1807, which used information supplied by people who had known the poet, says that Fergusson had contracted syphilis, and one cannot reject this outright, since Peterkin was a champion of Fergusson and wrote to defend him against what he considered unfair and uninformed criticism of his life. According to Peterkin's informant, it was while Fergusson was under the influence of medicine prescribed for his illness that "he was unfortunately enticed to accompany some gentlemen, who were interested in an election business, to one of the eastern counties of Scotland. On this expedition he was much exposed to the riotous enjoyments incident to such occasions; and these, in conjunction with his disordered health, produced a feverishness and decrepitude of mind amounting nearly to insanity."[5]

He was now very troubled by religious questions, moving, apparently, from scepticism about the doctrines of the Fall and vicarious atonement and their consistency with the wisdom and beneficence of God to self-torturing fears about his own entitlement to salvation and the future of his eternal soul. A few days in the nearby village of Restalrig did not soothe his mind, as expected, and he returned home more disturbed than ever. His condition was suddenly worsened by his being awakened one night by the screams of a starling that had been seized by a cat. According to George Gleig, whose account of Fergusson in the third edition of the *Encyclopedia Britannica* written at the very end of the eighteenth century derived from James Iverarity, contemplation of the fate of the starling "wrought his mind up to a pitch of remorse that almost bordered on frantic despair. Sleep now forsook his eyelids; and he rose in the morning, not as he had formerly done, to mix again with the social and gay, but to be a recluse from society, and to allow the remembrance of his past follies to prey upon his vitals."[6] A conversation he had had in the churchyard at Haddington with the minister Dr. John Brown about death and the last judgment now returned forcibly to his mind and intensified his religious despair. Alexander Campbell, in his *Introduction to the History of Scotch Poetry* (1798), says that Fergusson now burned all his manuscripts and confined himself henceforth to the reading of works of piety, notably Hervey's *Meditations Among the Tombs*.

In the summer of 1774 he appears to have made a recovery, and *The Caledonian Mercury* of 9 July referred to "the celebrated Rob. Fergusson, lately emerged from obscurity" and printed some verses by the actor William Woods welcoming him back to health: they were entitled "To Mr. R. Fergusson: On his Recovery". But on 28 July *The Mercury* announced that Fergusson "has been seized with a very dangerous illness". The early biographers, and Miss Ruddiman's information given to Grosart, says that in Grosart's words, "one night he had the misfortune to entangle his foot with a rod-knob, on the head of a staircase, and fell from it, striking his head violently against the lower steps. When lifted up and taken home he was utterly insensible."[7]

For two weeks after this Fergusson was under the care of Dr. Andrew Duncan, a fellow graduate of St. Andrews and a President of the Medical Faculty in Edinburgh. Dr. Duncan described how he found the poet:

I found him in a very deplorable condition, subjected to furious insanity. He lived in the house of his mother, an old Widow in very narrow circumstances. Her feeble and aged state, the situation of her dwelling-house, and several other circumstances, rendered it impossible to make any attempts towards cure, with the slightest prospect of advantage, while he remained at home. After several fruitless attempts to have him placed in a more desirable situation, he was at last removed to the Bedlam of the city of Edinburgh. There also I continued my visits to him, in conjunction with my late worthy friend Dr Alexander Wood ["Lang Sandie Wood", widely known and loved for his philanthropy and kindness], who had at that time charge of the Medical Department of the Edinburgh Poorhouse and of the Bedlam attached to it. Without a convalescence from his insanity, death soon put an end to poor Fergusson's existence.[8]

Dr. Duncan's pioneer work in the treatment of the mentally ill and his recognition of the need for providing adequate accommodation for them derived, as he himself recorded, from his involvement with Fergusson in his last days.

John Pinkerton, in his *Ancient Scottish Poems* (1786), gives a harrowing account of Fergusson's entry into Bedlam. He had been called on by two friends and induced to go into a sedan chair as though they were going to pay a social call. Pinkerton relates:

I was told by a person who was his most intimate friend, and who went to see him lodged there, as otherwise force alone could have carried him, that it was about nine o'clock at night when they went; and that the dismal habitation was quite silent: but upon Fergusson's entering the door he set up a strange halloo, which, in the instant, was repeated by the miserable inhabitants of all the cells in the house. My informant says, the sound was so horrible that he yet hears it.[9]

Thomas Somers records in his *Life of Robert Fergusson* (1803) that he, together with the surgeon Dr. John Aitken, visited the poet a few days before his death. "We got immediate access to the cell, and found Robert lying with his clothes on, stretched upon a bed of loose uncovered straw. The moment he heard my voice, he instantly arose—got me in his arms and wept."[10] He pleaded for his liberty, and Dr. Aitken, finding him in a reasonable mental state and not feverish, promised that he would soon be sent home. Campbell recorded that his mother visited him soon afterwards having received some money from her elder son Hary which would have enabled her to care for Robert more effectively at home. When it was time to lock the gates and for his mother to leave, he pleaded with her to stay. But she was not permitted to do so. Fergusson died that night, 17 October.

On 19 October Fergusson was buried in the Canongate Churchyard. The stone above his grave, which bears the commonly accepted but erroneous date of death 16 October instead of 17, was erected by Robert Burns when he was in Edinburgh in 1787.

Dr. Chalmers Davidson contributed a "Note on the Medical History of Robert Fergusson" to a collection of essays on the poet edited by Sydney Goodsir Smith in 1952. Having examined all the available biographical evidence and especially the accounts of his last weeks that have come down to us, Dr. Davidson concluded that in that final period Fergusson was "profoundly depressed and obsessed with feelings of guilt and unworthiness, symptoms typical of a manic depressive state which is frequently precipitated by the effects of a severe physical illness on a susceptible temperament. The prognosis in these cases is good, and there is little doubt that given modern care and treatment Fergusson would have recovered . . .. Although it would be unduly optimistic to assume that Fergusson's recovery would have been permanent, it would be reasonable to claim that he would have survived another fifteen years without a relapse. He would thus have been at the height of his powers when Robert Burns came to Edinburgh in 1787; inevitably they would have met, and the consequences to Scottish poetry of such an encounter provide a fascinating field for speculation."[11]

NOTES

1. Matthew P. McDiarmid, ed., *The Poems of Robert Fergusson*, Scottish Text Society, I, Edinburgh and London, 1954, p. 28.
2. Ibid., II, 1956, p. 257.
3. Robert Chambers, ed., *The Poetical Works of Robert Fergusson*, Edinburgh, 1840, p. 22.
4. A.B. Grosart, ed., *The Works of Robert Fergusson: With Life of the Author and an Essay on His Genius and Writings*, London, Edinburgh and Dublin, 1879, p. cvii.
5. Alexander Peterkin, ed., *The Works of Robert Fergusson, To Which is Prefixed, a Sketch of The Author's Life*, London, 1807, p. 70.
6. George Gleig, *Supplement to the Third Edition of the Encyclopedia Britannica*, I, Edinburgh, 1801, p. 648.
7. Grosart, *op. cit.*, p. xcv.
8. McDiarmid, *op. cit.*, p. 76.
9. Peterkin, *op. cit.*, p. cxl.
10. Thomas Somers, *The Life of Robert Fergusson, the Scottish Poet*, Edinburgh, 1803, p. 32.
11. Sydney Goodsir Smith, ed., *Robert Fergusson, the Scottish Poet*, Edin-Various Hands to Commemorate the Bicentenary of his Birth*, Edinburgh, 1952, p. 200.

CHAPTER IV

In 1779 Walter and Thomas Ruddiman published *Poems on Various Subjects. By Robert Fergusson. Part II.* "Part II" indicated that this volume was regarded as a sequel to the 1773 volume, to be sold together with it. (An advertisement in *The Edinburgh Advertiser* of 16 March 1779 announced the publication of the new volume and added: "Such as are possessed of the first part of these Poems, may be supplied with the second singly at 1s. 6d.") It also suggests that there were quite a number of unsold copies of the 1773 volume still available. The new volume contained seventeen poems in Scots and sixteen in English, all of which except one had appeared in *The Weekly Magazine*. Some of the English poems are very brief epitaphs and epigrams. The volume also contained the "Epistle to Robert Fergusson" by J. S. The Scots poems came first, a reversal of the 1773 order, presumably indicating that Fergusson was here presented as primarily a Scots poet. There was also a third section, of "Posthumous Pieces", of which the most interesting is a version in Scots octosyllabic couplets of the eleventh ode of Book I of Horace's Odes. The other poems in this section are in English—a brief, sad poem in octosyllables entitled "The Author's Life", obviously the product of his depression; an uninspired eight-line song beginning "Since brightest beauty soon must fade"; a curious "Ode to Disappointment" in an English rhetorical style but in the "Standart *Habby*" stanza; an "Ode to Horror", a rhetorical moralising poem in octosyllables; a fourteen-line poem "On Night", also in octosyllables, an exercise in graveyard moodiness; and a

paraphrase in heroic couplets of the third chapter of the
Book of Job, beginning "Perish the fatal day when I was
born", again obviously the product of his depression, but
done with some skill and vigour.

There were some poems of Fergusson's that were
published in neither the 1773 nor the 1774 volume. One is
a re-writing of an old song, and shows Fergusson in the
role, unusual for him and more associated with Ramsay
and Burns, of refurbisher of folk poetry. It first appeared
in a collection of songs called *The Charmer* in 1782. It is in
four stanzas of four lines, beginning

> Will ye gang o'er the lee-rigg
>   My ain kind deary O!
> And cuddle there sae kindly
>   Wi' me, my kind deary O?

The final stanza goes

> While others herd their lambs and ewes,
>   And toil for warld's gear, my jo,   goods
> Upon the lee my pleasure grows,
>   Wi' you, my kind dearie O!

The song in its various late eighteenth-century printings
was entitled sometimes "The Lee Rigg" and sometimes
"My ain kind dearie O". Though never publicly
attributed to Fergusson, the evidence of his authorship is
convincing. Burns knew it, and admired it, as
Fergusson's. The last stanza would have particularly
appealed to Burns, with its disdain of "warld's gear" in
favour of amorous pleasure. It is—except perhaps for the
phrase "my pleasure grows" which does not quite have
the folk ring—a simple and effective song in the folk tradition. We know that Fergusson liked to sing such songs, but
he did not normally write them. His other songs are in
neo-classic English.

The one poem in the 1779 volume, except for those in
the section of Posthumous Pieces, that had not appeared

in *The Weekly Magazine* is the fine Scots poem "Auld Reikie". This had been published separately in 1773, as "Auld Reekie, A Poem. Canto I", and after its 328 lines in octosyllabic couplets we find END OF CANTO I. The 1779 volume prints this first canto together with a further forty lines that wind up a poem originally intended as a much longer piece in several cantos. It seems to have been lack of encouragement that led Fergusson to change his plan. The one surviving copy of the poem in its original edition has no dedication, but A.B. Grosart reported that he had seen a copy with a dedication reading: "To Sir William Forbes, Baronet, this poem is most respectfully dedicated, by his most obedient and very humble servant, the Author."[1] Forbes, banker, author, member of Dr. Johnson's literary Club, was one of the best known and influential Scots of his day, and in dedicating his poem to him Fergusson was following the accepted method of trying to get important support for his claims as a poet. David Irving asserted that the great man refused to accept the compliment, so that the dedication was cancelled from other copies.[2] If this were so, it would explain how Fergusson became discouraged and abandoned his more ambitious plan for the poem.

"Auld Reikie" shows how splendidly Fergusson could adapt the tradition of octosyllabic couplets developed by English poets—Butler, Swift, Prior, Gay, among others—to vigorous Scots local poetry. This is the Edinburgh poet's fullest and most accomplished celebration of his city. The couplets, shifting in tempo in accordance with the particular scene before the poet's eye, carry the expressive Scots forcefully to the ear, while the imagery, fixing the scene with its most significant component or appropriate symbol, builds up the Edinburgh sights, sounds and smells. This is more than a Dickensian exploration of urban oddities or the search for the striking scene or incident: the whole poem is set in a framework of acceptance—acceptance of the whole of life, with its

colour, gaiety and debauchery, dreariness and pre-
tentiousness and weakness, companionship, loneliness
and sheer unadulterated humanity. He is not exhibiting
Edinburgh to a sniggering or an admiring audience; he is
savouring its full quality because he enjoys doing so. The
whole Edinburgh scene passes under his eye. Gossips,
schoolboys, housemaids, lawyers, thieves, whores, tavern-
hunters, Sunday walkers, corrupt politicians, each
against their appropriate background, are picked out and
described; and there is an under-current of satire directed
against those who through laziness or selfishness neglect
the city's welfare or actively contribute to its harm.

The poem opens by setting the late autumn scene in the
city. But though the winter winds will blow, the high tene-
ments of the Old Town, built by our ancestors, will shelter
us from the cold north and east winds:

best; every	AULD REIKIE, wale o' ilka town
	That *Scotland* kens beneath the moon;
sociable-fellows	Whare couthy chiels at e'ening meet
parched throats and mouths make	Their bizzing *craigs* and *mous* to weet;
	And blythly gar auld care gae bye
tipsy	Wi' blinkit and wi' bleering eye:
	O'er lang frae thee the Muse has been
	Sae frisky on the *Simmer*'s green,
daisies; gleam	What flowers and gowans wont to glent
glances; field	In bonny blinks upo' the bent;
	But now the *leaves* of yellow dye,
	Peel'd frae the *branches*, quickly fly;
	And now frae nouther bush nor brier
song-thrush	The spreckl'd *mavis* greets your ear;
	Nor bonny blackbird *skims* and *roves*
	To seek his love in yonder groves.
	Then *Reikie*, welcome! Thou canst charm
undismayed	Unfleggit by the year's alarm;
keenly	Not Boreas, that sae snelly blows,

Dare here pap in his angry nose:
Thanks to our *dads*, whase biggin stands   building
A shelter to surrounding lands.

The barefoot housemaids stand on the stairs ready to
empty their pails of slop below:

On stair we' *tub*, or *pat* in hand,   pot
The barefoot *housemaids* loe to stand,
That antrin fock may ken how *snell*   folk met by chance; sharp
Auld Reikie will at *morning smell*:
Then, with an *inundation big* as
The *burn* that 'neath the *Nor' Loch*
   brig is,   bridge
They kindly shower EDINA's roses,
To *quicken* and *regale* our noses.

The "stair-head critics, senseless fools" find fault with
their neighbours. The sun comes up, noon approaches,
schoolboys come out for their "noon-day play", lawyers
and tradesmen display themselves at the Mercat Cross,
talking of their affairs. As evening approaches, the scene
changes to one of varied conviviality. The contrasts are
frequent and impressive:

Near some lamp-post, wi' dowy face,   gloomy
Wi' heavy ein, and sour grimace,   eyes
Stands she that beauty lang had kend,
Whoredom her trade, and vice her end.
But see whare now she wuns her bread
By that which nature ne'er decreed;
And sings sad music to the lugs,   ears
'Mang bourachs o' damn'd whores and
   rogues.
Whane'er we reputation lose,
Fair chastity's transparent gloss!
Redemption seenil kens the name,   seldom
But a's black misery and shame.

Drunks reel out of taverns. At ten o'clock some convivial characters continue drinking, some go home to their wives, some go to their wenches. Later we get an account of the altered scene on a Sunday:

finely dressed

In afternoon, a' brawlie buskit,
The joes and lasses loe to frisk it:
Some tak a great delight to place
The modest *bon-grace* o'er the face;
Tho' you may see, if so inclin'd,
The turning o' the leg behind.
Now Comely-garden, and the Park,
Refresh them, after forenoon's wark;
Newhaven, Leith, or Canon-mills,
Supply them in their Sunday's gills;
Whare writers aften spend their pence,
To stock their heads wi' drink and sense.

The poet himself prefers to take his afternoon walk by Arthur's Seat, "Whare bonny Pastures meet the View": the sense of the countryside being very close to the city and even intermingled with it comes out strongly in the poem. Or if it rains he might go to Holyrood and muse on history, lamenting the decay of the old "domicile of ancient kings". He reproaches the Duke of Hamilton, the hereditary keeper of the palace, for his neglect of it:

sociable
heed

O HAMILTON, for shame! the muse
Would pay to thee her couthy vows,
Gid ye wad tent the humble strain,
And gie's our dignity again.

The patriotic note, with an underlying implication of the sad consequences of the Union of 1707, recurs again and again in Fergusson's poetry.

The poem pays eloquent tribute to George Drummond, six times Lord Provost of Edinburgh, who during his twelve years in office was closely associated with the development of the New Town and the improvement of

the face of the city. He had died in 1766 and did not live to
see the emergence of the New Town of Edinburgh in all its
glory, though the vision had been his. Fergusson, though
essentially an Old Town man, saw the New Town
developing as he moved about the city and realised what
the new developments would mean.

> Peace to thy shade, thou wale o'   best
>   men,
> DRUMMOND! relief to poortith's   poverty's
>   pain:
> To thee the greatest bliss we owe,
> And tribute's tear shall grateful flow:
> The sick are cur'd, the hungry fed,
> And dreams of comfort 'tend their bed:
> As lang as *Forth* weets *Lothian*'s shore,
> As lang's on *Fife* her billows roar,
> Sae lang shall ilk whase country's   everyone
>   dear,
> To thy remembrance gie a tear.
> By thee *Auld Reikie* thrave and grew
> Delightfu' to her childer's view:
> Nae mair shall *Glasgow* striplings
>   threep   boast
> Their city's beauty and its shape,
> While our new city spreads around
> Her bonny wings on fairy ground.

It is interesting that Fergusson sees the new development
as enabling Edinburgh to vie with Glasgow in beauty, a
reminder that the industrial Glasgow of the next century
was still to come. He goes on to lament the corruption that
delayed the construction of the North Bridge and
produced the collapse of its south end in 1769.

The conclusion, where the poet retires across the Forth
to look at his city whole, across the water from Fife, rounds
the poem off perfectly, in spite of the fact that it was not
Fergusson's original intention to end at this point. He has

packed into the poem social observations, satire, compliment, evocation of atmosphere, personal feeling, moral
precepts, and much else, but everything is carried by the
steady yet varied flow of the verse. The Scots octosyllabic
couplet as Fergusson used it here is a supple and expressive medium, responsive to the varying scenes and moods
the poet wishes to convey. The result is an altogether different kind of urban picture from, say, Eliot's evocation of
London at the end of Part I of "The Waste Land" or
Baudelaire's vision of Paris that influenced Eliot—

> Fourmillante cité, cité pleine de rêves,
> Où le spectre en plein jour raccroche le passant.

Fergusson's is a much more concrete kind of poetry. Not
only is he part of what he describes, sharing the humanity
of his Edinburgh's citizens however much he may censure
or deplore some of them; he is also addressing an audience
who shares his participation. It is true, as Sydney Goodsir
Smith pointed out, that "there is a metropolitan flavour
about Fergusson's satire that was a product of his city
breeding and classical education—an ambience quite
outside the experience of the 'rustic Bard,' as Burns
romantically but quite correctly called himself."[3] But it is
also true that Fergusson saw Edinburgh in its context,
often looking at it across the Forth from Fife, seeing its surrounding fields and hills. He was an urban poet with a
strong sense of the impact of the country on the city and of
the relation between age-old rustic celebrations, relating
to the farmer's year, and urban conviviality. This was
partly because of his own nature and experience, and
partly because of the nature of Edinburgh in his time. (We
have taken the text of "Auld Reikie" in the quotations
above from the 1779 volume and not from the 1773
edition. There is less unnecessary capitalizing (though
correspondingly more italicising) in the 1779 text, which
is as a result more appealing to the modern reader.)
       Another poem that never appeared in *The Weekly*

Magazine is that entitled simply "Dumfries". This com-
memorates a visit Fergusson paid to Dumfries—travelling
there on foot with a friend—in 1773, and it first appeared
in *The Dumfries Weekly Magazine* for 28 September 1773. It
is a poem in the "Standart *Habby*" stanza celebrating and
complimenting the town, and especially the opportunities
for conviviality that it afforded. It is especially interesting
for the easy and confident way in which Fergusson
introduces classical allusions into his Scots speech:

> Had Horace liv'd, that pleasant sinner,
> That loo'd gude wine to synd his dinner,   wash down
> His muse tho' douf, the de'il be in her,   melacholy
>   She'd lous'd her tongue,
> The drink cou'd round Parnassus rin her
>   In blythest sang.

> Nae mair he'd sung to auld Maecenas,
> The blinking ein o' bonny Venus,   shining eyes
> His leave o' them he'd ta'en at anis   once
>   For Claret here,
> Which Jove and a' his Gods still rain us
>   Frae year to year.

> O Jove, man, gie's some orrow pence,   spare
> Mair sillar, an' a wie mair sense,   money
> I'd big to you a rural spence,   build; room
>   An' bide a' simmer,   remain
> An' cald frae saul and body fence
>   With frequent brimmer.

Horace, "that pleasant sinner", "auld Maecenas",
"bonny Venus", "O Jove, man"—these friendly, not to
say intimate, references to classical characters and deities
represent a kind of appropriation of the classical world
that no other Scottish poet of the century was capable of.

"Dumfries" shows, as so many of Fergusson's Scots

poems do, what A.D. Mackie has called "the variety and elasticity" of the poet's Scots. "Here you have a fine old language in all its moods—racy one moment, genteel the next, rough and graceful by turns, lowbrow and highbrow both."[4] Fergusson's best Scots poems combine craftsmanship and *ease*. This is surprising if one considers the state of Scots in Fergusson's day. It was not any more a full-blooded language, but had become a series of regional dialects. Fergusson took the Scots of the Edinburgh streets, enriched it with English in varying degrees, intermixed the Edinburgh Scots with Scots from other regions, notably the north-east, and also with an older Scots learned from Watson and the poems in *The Evergreen* as well as certain of Ramsay's archaising Scots poems, and made the amalgam work with supreme self-confidence. He could, like the mediaeval Scots makars, use Scots and English versions of a word in the same poem, because of the exigencies of rhyme or the expressive demands of the poem at a given point. The inconsistency adds richness not confusion. There is perhaps some confusion in his adopting Ramsay's habit of spelling Scots as though it were delinquent English, with abundance of apostrophes, but this orthographical habit has had a long history and Fergusson is far from the only culprit. When one considers how short his life was and the fact that virtually all his poetry was written within the space of two years, his achievement appears quite remarkable. One must consider too his enormous influence on Burns, for whom the encounter with Fergusson's poems was crucial in his poetic development, as he emphatically stated in his autobiographical letter to Dr. John Moore. Many of Burns's poems of celebration and description—indeed, nearly all of the kinds of poems he wrote except the songs—show some of Fergusson's influence. It would be a lengthy business to go through Burns and point out the echoes of Fergusson both in particular phrases and in general patterns and topics.[5]

NOTES

1. A. B. Grosart, ed., *The Workds of Robert Fergusson: With Life of the Author and an Essay of His Genius and Writings*, London, Edinburgh and Dublin, 1879, p. 126.
2. David Irving, *The Lives of the Scottish Poets*, Edinburgh, 1804, p. 433.
3. Sydney Goodsir Smith, ed., *Robert Fergusson 1750–1774*, Edinburgh, 1952, p. 34.
4. *Ibid.*, p. 146.
5. In his Scottish Text Society edition of Fergusson's poems, Matthew McDiarmid identifies details of Burns's debt to Fergusson in notes to individual poems, and, in his general account of the poetry, gives a list of the poems that show the most conspicuous debts (I, 182).

CHAPTER V

Fergusson's reputation has been eclipsed by that of Burns, and most students of Scottish literature know him as Burns's predecessor rather than as a Scots poet in his own right. The trio of "Ramsay, Fergusson and Burns" has long figured in standard accounts of what happened in Scottish poetry in the eighteenth century, with the suggestion—or even the explicit statement—that the former two were forerunners of Burns and chiefly significant for that reason. Burns himself would have modestly agreed. When, in his verse epistle to William Simpson of Ochiltree, he expressed his ambition to celebrate his own part of Scotland, it was to emulate what Ramsay and Fergusson had done for theirs:

> Ramsay an' famous Fergusson
> Gied Forth an' Tay a lift aboon;
> Yarrow an' Tweed, to monie a tune,
>   Owre Scotland rings;
> While Irwin, Lugar, Ayr, an' Doon
>   Naebody sings.

Earlier in the same poem he expressed his ambition to do as well as Ramsay, William Hamilton of Gilbertfield and Fergusson:

> My senses wad be in a creel,
> Should I but dare a hope to speel,
> Wi' Allan, or wi' Gilbertfield,
>   The braes o' fame;
> Or Fergusson, the writer-chiel,
>   A deathless name.

He clearly regarded Fergusson as the greatest of his predecessors. After the mention of him in this stanza he added another stanza in parenthesis:

> (O Fergusson! thy glorious parts
> Ill suited law's dry, musty arts!
> My curse upon your whunstane hearts
>   Ye E'nbrugh gentry!
> The tythe o' what ye waste at cartes
>   Wad stow'd his pantry!)

Burns regarded Fergusson as a poet driven to his death by the unfeeling disregard of his contemporaries, as he made clear in his epitaph on him:

> Curse on ungrateful man, that can be pleas'd
> And yet can starve the author of the pleasure!

> O thou, my elder brother in Misfortune,
> By far my elder Brother in the muse,
> With tears I pity thy unhappy fate!
> Why is the Bard unfitted for the world,
> Yet has so keen a relish of its Pleasures?

After Fergusson's death *The Weekly Magazine* continued for a while to publish poems in Scots, but found no real successor to the dead poet. Charles Keith produced in his poem "Written extempore to a young Gentleman, on his getting a CLOAK and WIG" an imitation of Fergusson's "Braid Claith" (*Weekly Magazine*, 8 December 1774) and three weeks later there appeared his imitation of "The Farmer's Ingle" entitled "The Farmer's Ha'", in Buchan Scots. Another poet showing strong Fergusson influence whose work appeared in *The Weekly Magazine* after Fergusson's death was John Mayne, whose poems include "Hallow E'en", "On the Return of March" and "Glasgow: a Poem", all published in the early 1780s. In a poem entitled "To the Publishers of the Weekly Magazine", which appeared in the magazine on 17 April

1779, Mayne described the reception of Fergusson's poems as they appeared week by week:

> Blyth hae I seen about the ingle
> The neighbours a', baith wed and single,
> Flock round, to hear his verses jingle
>   Frae far and near,
> The priest wad aft amang them mingle
>   An lean to hear.

This is fairly typical of the "Standart *Habby*" poems turned out by Keith and Mayne under Fergusson's influence. They, like so many critics who wrote just after Fergusson's death, regarded him as a lively and amusing Scots poet of urban life and did not recognize the unique qualities of his poetry. "The subjects he generally chose," wrote Thomas Ruddiman in his obituary notice, "were generally uncommon, even temporary", and he selected "Hallow-Fair", "The Election" and "Leith Races" as poems illustrative of Fergusson's talent at its best.

There was considerable interest shown in Fergusson's life in the decades after his death. A short sketch of his life by Thomas Ruddiman appeared in the 1799 volume of the poems, and this was several times reprinted. David Irving edited the poems, with a biography, in 1799 and Alexander Peterkin did the same in 1807. Irving returned to Fergusson in 1801 with his *Lives of Scottish Authors: Viz. Fergusson, Falconer, And Russell* and again in 1804 in his *Lives of the Scottish Poets.* Thomas Somers published his biography in 1803. The poems themselves were reprinted in 1782 (about 7,000 printed and sold), 1785 (again about 7,000), 1788–9 (Perth), 1796 (Paisley), 1799 (Edinburgh), 1800 (St. Andrews), 1802 (Alnwick, with engravings by Bewick), and at fairly regular intervals until Alexander B. Grosart's important edition, with notes and biography based on papers now lost and considerable original research, in 1851. This suggests that, in spite of the fact that Fergusson was considered chiefly as a forerunner of Burns, there was a steady if limited interest in his poems up to the middle of the nineteenth century. The next edition after Grosart's was Robert Aiken's in 1895, followed by Robert Ford's in 1905: both contained biographies derived from earlier published material.

The nineteenth century tradition was that Fergusson lived a dissipated life and died young as a result. R. L. Stevenson, who felt himself so close to Fergusson that in some respects he saw himself as a reincarnation of the eighteenth-century poet, nevertheless regarded him as "the poor, white-faced, drunken, vicious boy that raved himself to death in the Edinburgh madhouse". Writing from Samoa to W. Craibe Angus, he expressed a wish that more would be "gleaned about Fergusson" and went on to associate himself with both Fergusson and Burns:

> We are three Robins who have touched the Scots lyre this last century. Well the one is the world's, he did it, he came off, he is for ever: but I and the other—ah! what bonds we have—born in the same city: both sickly, both pestered one nearly to madness, one to the madhouse with a damnatory creed; both seeing the stars and the dawn, and wearing shoe-leather on the same ancient stones, under the same pends, down the same closes, where our common ancestors clashed in their armour, rusty or bright. And the old Robin, who was before Burns and the flood, died in his acute, painful youth, and left the models of the great things that were to come; and the new, who came after, outlived his green-sickness, and has faintly tried to parody the finished work. If you will collect the strays of Robin Fergusson, fish for material, collect any last re-echoing of gossip, command me to do what you prefer—to write the preface—to write the whole if you prefer: anything, so that another monument (after Burns's) be set up to my unhappy predecessor on the causey of Auld Reekie. You will never know, nor will any man, how deep this feeling is: I believe Fergusson lives in me.

The first suggestion of a new interest in Fergusson deriving from or associated with the Scottish poetic renaissance of the twentieth century can perhaps be seen in Bruce Dickins' edition of the *Scots Poems* that appeared in 1925, the same year as the publication of Hugh MacDiarmid's *Sangschaw*. A firmer indication of new interest is found in the collection of essays on Fergusson edited by the Scots poet Sydney Goodsir Smith and published in 1952. The two-volume edition of Fergusson's poems edited by Matthew P. McDiarmid for the Scottish Text Society in 1954–6 marks the establishment of Fergusson as a Scottish poetic classic but not as a widely popular poet in Scotland, least of all anywhere else. Fergusson's influence on twentieth-century Scottish poets, notably on Sydney Smith and, even more significantly, on Robert Garioch—who is the poet of twentieth-century Edinburgh as Fergusson was of eighteenth-century Edinburgh—is the most living proof of his continued significance. One of the classic Scots poems of our time is Garioch's poem, "At Robert Fergusson's Grave, October 1962", which can stand as the poet's modern epitaph:

Canongait kirkyaird in the falling
    year

rose-bushes

is auld and grey, the wee roseirs are
    bare,

gleam

five gulls leam white agin the dirty
    air:
why are they here? There's naething
    for them here.

Why are we here oursels? We gaither
    near
the grave. Fergussons mainly, quite
    a fair
turn-out, respectfu, ill at ease, we
    stare

at daith—there's an address—I canna
hear.

Aweill, we staund bareheidit in the
    haar,
murnin a man that gaed back til the
    pool
twa-hunner year afore our time. The
    glaur   mud

    that haps his banes glowres back.   covers;
    Strang, present dool   grief
ruggs at my hairt. Lichtlie this gin   tugs; make light of; if
    ye daur:
here Robert Burns knelt and kissed the
    mool.   earth

NOTES

1. Sidney Colvin, ed., *The Letters of Robert Louis Stevenson to his Family and Friends*, New York, 1899, II, p. 266.
2. Robert Garioch, *Collected Poems*, Loanhead 1977, p. 130.